LESSONS FOR MY GRANDCHILDREN

I dedicate this work to:
Elvia Strutzel, Beatriz Gerdts, Veronica Rubio, Marco Egoavil Jr, Dan Strutzel, Andres Rubio, and Brian Perrin.

A special thanks to the editor and illustrator of this book, my sixteen year old granddaughter Ariana Rubio, who studies at Latymer Upper School in London.

CONTENTS:

An Introductory Message from the Author

Everyone has a grandfather. I would have liked to learn all of the lessons my grandparents could have given to me, so this book is for my grandchildren- or, indeed, anyone else who has a grandfather like me: an engineer, teacher, sportsman. I was never famous, nor rich, but I thank God every day for the life he has given me. My wealth in this world are my four children, eleven grandchildren, and two great-grandchildren; who all make me feel like a millionaire. This book is first and foremost for my family, who I hope will regard their time reading well spent. My mother, from whom I inherited my small stature and short-sightedness, died when I was seven years old. From my father, I inherited patience and easy sleep. My children often joke about how I fall asleep anywhere, and my grandchildren prod me to see if I'm dead. From both of my parents I inherited perseverance, ambition, the love of study and work, and the heart of a sportsman who always like to win. I was blessed in childhood with six siblings, of which Marina, Efraim, and Carlos have been called by God, may they rest in peace. My primary education was completed at the Colegio Peruano de los Sagrados Corazones in Barranco; and my Aunt Carlota Suarez was the Principle. I finished primary school at the Colegio America of Callao. My math teacher, Miss Cameron, first taught me the elegant discipline of study; which later formed the foundation of my career as an engineer. I learnt to pray during the 1940 earthquake in Callao. Education has always been very important to me; I got a degree in Mechanical Engineering from the National University of Engineering in Lima, Peru, in 1954. I am a ME54, as we rather proudly if deservedly call ourselves. My shyness was tested to the utmost degree throughout my fifteen ear membership of the Toast-Masters international club— I learnt how to speak in public the hard way! I got a Master's degree and doctorate in Mechanical Engineering from the University of Notre Dame (South bend, Indiana) where my first-born daughter later attended university. I was a Professor of Thermodynamics, employed at the NASA Langley Research Centre in Hampton, Virginia, as an Aerospace Technologist. It was there that I learnt to play tennis. As an old man I played with my granddaughter, determined not to let my age deter me, and I played soccer at sixty with my coworkers. The girl in red, who lived in Chucuito, was my first platonic love. I first experienced love of the romantic variation when I met a certain Colombian lady named Elvia Duque, whom I am fortunate enough to have married. Unfortunately, I had not yet conquered my shyness, and proposed by letter; much to the amusement of my grandchildren. God blessed my wife and I with three beautiful daughters and a wonderful son. My daughters gifted me further with the eleven grandchildren for whom this book is intended. I learnt to play tennis as a professor. As an old man, I played with my granddaughter, determined not to let age deter me; at sixty years old I still played soccer with my coworkers. I retired from NASA in 2002 and moved to West Palm Beach, Florida, where I wrote this book and would play tennis every day with friends. I changed residence, where I could not find any adequate partners, though my granddaughter makes a very good partner when she visits. As a student, I learnt countless lessons, yet my years as a teacher taught me more. I understood from an early age that education is everything, and if this were the only advice I could give to my grandchildren, I would be content. The main advice I would like to give to my grandchildren and to the children of Africa, Asia, India, Australia, Europe, and South and North America is that all of them should go to university to get a degree, and to aim to get a Ph. D. A university degree is an invaluable asset in life, and I hope that many of them will go on to obtain Master's degrees, or even doctorates, as I did. Education is everything, or at least, nearly.

Marco Egoavil Suarez
West Palm Beach, January 2019
Learning in Life

CHAPTER ONE: LESSONS FROM SPORTS

My dad gave me my first soccer ball on my third birthday. I could hardly hold it, but that rubber ball was the most beloved of all my toys. When I was seven, we would play a game called Bata during recess, which is similar in principle to softball, but you used your hand as a hitter. I would team up with my sister Milagro and brother Cesar, we were an unbeatable team. It was then that I first learned the value of winning, and believed that it was engraved in my hands, in my feet. Perhaps because of the fun I had with my siblings then, that I felt that I should always win. I didn't feel any disappointment then, for we hardly ever lost a game. That theory was discredited the day I turned ten years old. My Aunt Carlota gave me a number three leather soccer ball, and I kicked the stuffing out of that ball. For five years, my brothers Efraim, Cesar, Carlos, and never less than four cousins, would go every afternoon to play at a field two blocks from our house. One day, we challenged some boys about our age to a game. We agreed that the victor would be the first team to score five goals. The other team had three very good dribblers; even Cesar and I, the best of our team, couldn't out-dribble the other boys despite our best efforts. Soon, they won. Not wanting to accept defeat, I suggested we play to seven. They soon won that as well. I learnt that sometimes you must accept loss. In fact, it makes victory even greater. Always must we want to win,

but there will always be someone slightly better than you.
Win and be humble, lose and be humble; is my motto. As
the great Rafael Nadal does after losing a match, shake
hands and congratulate the winner, and know that on that
day they deserved victory more than you.

**Lesson One: In all aspects of your life, be humble when
winning and humble when losing.**

CHAPTER TWO: SPORTS LESSONS

I entered my secondary school, Callao High School, when I was twelve years of age. My professor of Physical Education was Cesar Garcia. On the first day of school, he would measure all us boys. Those who were tall grinned smugly, some had grown five centimeters, others four, and one pupil grew twelve centimeters! When it was my turn, my teacher told me: Marco, you grew one centimeter. The others laughed, but I understood that God had predestined me to be short. One teacher, Mr Belevan, who I recall had a rather wide moustache, would take us to a stadium to practice sports. One day, we had to execute car wheels; and I was excited because I knew how to roll car wheels— and I knew I was good. Showing off a bit, I tried to do a third consecutive car wheel and fell face-first into the grass. Everyone laughed, but my teacher helped me up. He understood that I had made an effort to impress him, and he appreciated that. It matters more how much effort and time you put into something, than your natural ability. During a theoretical class, Mr Belevan told us that we were going to play softball. For the first time, there would be a team captain who would have the great responsibility of choosing teammates. To my surprise, and the surprise of the other students, he said: Marco will be team captain. I suspect that the car rolling incident influenced his decision. That event marked my career as a leader. I spoke with potential players, and put together the team that was to compete against another school in the national stadium. My brother Efraim asked me to include him, and I nearly said no. But I conceded, because he was my brother and you must always help your own family before others. You are indebted to their love, and owe them love in turn. During the game in Lima, I was short stop, and the best move I made was to catch a ball and get the opposing player out. We didn't win, but I reminded myself that losing isn't shameful. And, I was so happy with my move it felt like I had won. You can't suddenly leap to success, there must be stepping stones that are equally worth celebrating. During my third year in secondary school, we were informed that we must choose between Secondary Commercial (to begin working right after school) or Secondary Regular (to go to university). I was one of the ten students who opted for Secondary Regular, the other thirty boys chose Secondary Commercial. This meant that my class could only play in a few sports, as we only had six good athletes. Juan Barrera, who grew 12 cm the first year was one of the best athlete because he was already 1.81 m tall. I was at the other end, as my height at that time was 1.54 m. The other good athletes in my class were José Alegre and Luis Lyons, whom I believe studied medicine in the USA. There was an athletics competition in the Bellavista Stadium, and each lass was to submit four athletes to compete against the other classes. However, only I and Hector Chumpitazi could compete. The teacher consulted the other teams, and they decided we could compete as a team of two in the 4x50 relay. A boy named Bobby Carbajo told us: 'we are going to remove your casings.' I started the race, and my opponent drew five meters ahead of me at the first changing of the baton. But my teammate Hector, who later went on to become National Champion in the 100 meter dash easily won the race for us by about 25 meters. The other team had lost by so much because their changing of the batons were slow and cumbersome. They protested, claiming that it was not fair, but the teacher gave us the medals of the winners. The other team learnt, and we also learnt that to compete you must be careful and cunning. My advice is that if you are going to compete in something that you think you good at, prepare yourself and create a game plan. This idea is reinforced by a game of chess I played and which is described below: My teacher Mr Beleván organized competitions between classes and schools throughout the year, including chess. My debut as a chess player was very successful because I applied the Spanish saying: "Mas vale mana que fuerza," which means : "Better use your brains than your force". The day of the competition our chess representative Pedro Medelius became ill and everyone asked: "Who knows how to play chess? ". I said I could, but I had never played in a tournament before. He convinced me to do my best and just show up at the competition as the representative of our class. I knew that my opponent was good, so I came up with a strategy. I would take my opponent's pieces and in turn let him take mine. This, I reasoned, would disorientate him. Halfway through the game Ernesto Balli, a senior student, approached us and declared that the blacks were very well positioned, and would likely win. Of course, I had the white pieces. Undeterred, I proceeded to try out my strategy. Soon, we had no horses, no bishops, no pawns- I had spoiled any good moves my opponent could have made. With a Tower and a Queen I became anxious- I could say checkmate. After clearing my throat I said the magic words, and that was a big win for me. I learnt that even if one is the underdog there is always a way to win if you have a plan. Even for friendly games of tennis I always prepared a game plan. You have to apply this principle to your problems: always prepare and present yourself with a game plan. For example, in school plan to get good grades, and then think about which career to pursue at university. I will write extensively upon the topic of universities, the most important topic, later in this book.

Lesson Two: Even if you're the underdog in a competition, there is always a way to win if you have a plan for the game.

CHAPTER THREE: THE POWER OF PRAY

My ccousin Armando, nicknamed Mano, and I were leaving school one day in May of 1940, when we heard a strange and distant sound. Looking around, we saw no airplane, no train, nothing. Suddenly, the ground began to move, and we quickly ran to the centre of the street- the window glass was falling down. Everyone was screaming in fear, with terror in their eyes, and were shouting: 'Earthquake, earthquake!'. A thick dust fell from the roofs of houses, and people were rushing by me. Not knowing what to do, I started running, too. I saw a lady dressed in black, kneeling, her hands clasped together in tender prayer. I ran closer; and saw the serenity of her face, as though it were momentarily graced by the divinity to which she prayed. Her lips were moving, and she emulated a calm emotion— and as suddenly as the earthquake had come my fears were gone. It was then that I learnt the power of prayer, and that in moments of fear and despair one should pray. I understood even better this notion years later when I was involved in a car accident. I was travelling in a shared taxi to Lima, in order to take an English class. I was seated next to the driver, and directly to my left a young lady. Those taxi's travelled at about 100km/hour. Whilst passing a cemetery, I happened to glance forwards and noticed that a car was accelerating directly opposite us. Almost immediately, I felt the impact of the two cars crashing nose on nose, and I lost consciousness. Days later, my family informed me that someone had held and dragged me from the car to the sidewalk. My face was all bloodied, and someone wrapped my head in my shirt to stop the bleeding. Someone pointed at me said-"This one is dead,wait no, no he is talking ". Another said-"No, he isn't crying, he's praying". Even unconscious I remembered that in moments of pain you must pray. Now I think that because of my prayers God returned to me my life, and thanks to those prayers that I can now write this story. They took me to the Bellavista Hospital and it was due to my dad's insistence that the next day I was moved into the Bellavista Clinic. I was unconscious and comatose for twenty-three hours laying on my back. I finally opened my eyes in front of the unshaven face of my father who was checking if I was still breathing. He cried for the doctor, and told him I had woken up. The plastic surgery on my forehead gave me a wide scar, and I also had a cut just under my lip, which caused my politically inclined brother Reynaldo to remark 'Now you won't be able to kiss any girls!'. The next week, I was still in bed with my left foot plastered up to my knee. On my twentieth day in the clinic, my cousin Amanda visited. We were talking quietly in my room, when again I heard that strange and distant nose. The room was on the second floor, and the building began to shake. Amanda immediately jumped up, but I yelled:

'No, don't go, kneel down and pray, pray.' I began to pray the Our Father in a loud voice. Astonished, Amanda looked at me, and later told me that when she saw me praying without fear, she calmed down and learnt the lesson: in moments of pain and fear one should pray. She witnessed the power of prayer. To further describe the power of prayer I will now jump to 2009 in Orlando, Florida, where a niece of my wife Elvia was diagnosed with leukaemia. Her name is also Elvia Maria. She received chemotherapy and radiation treatments, which stopped the disease, but throughout the following eight months she still had problems with reductions in haemoglobin and white blood cells. The doctors decided to give her a blood marrow transplant, and her sister Maria provided the marrow. Elvia Maria comes from a religious family since her uncle Aristobulo Duque was the parish priest in the village where almost all of the Duque brothers were born. Father Aristóbulo was later moved to a church in Cartagena. Elvia Maria's aunt, Sister Rubelia Duque González, of the Congregation of Dominican Sisters of Charity of the Presentation, created in 1988 in Cali, Colombia, CREAN aimed to improve the quality of life of elderly people in vulnerable situations and bring them back to their families. Grandparents receive visitors of CREAN in their homes, as well as support in health, recreation, food and living with their families. The main priority was enrolling the elderly to the system of identification of potential beneficiaries of social programs, so that they have access to the health service and to a monetary government assistance. Along the way, this project has joined different organisations and recruited people who work, commit, and contribute greatly to improve the lives of older adults. Sister Rubelia is passionate about the elderly's right to be accompanied, protected, and looked after. The foundation, which today helps three hundred and fifty people, is supported by organisations such as the Institute for the Blind and Deaf, and Colanta & Kuty Bakery. Returning to Elvia Maria, she never tired of praying, and she felt in all of her being that God would cure her disease. One evening, she prayed with such intensity and faith that she relaxed, and a wave of heat darted from her head to toes, and she felt a sudden strength in her muscles. This all happened so quickly that she payed no attention, and calmly continued praying. Next day she went to the doctor's in order to have her daily blood analysis and checkup. After studying the results, the doctor called Elvia Maria and said:

'Why, you're lab results are almost perfect! What have you done? Your hemoglobin is normal, though the leukocytes may not be better. It seems a miracle that you have recovered so unexpectedly.' Inside, Elvia Maria wept. She realized that God must have healed her the other day when she felt the heat wave. Soon, she was crying tears of joy and faith and utter gratitude, and thanking God.When I was member of the NASA Toastmasters Club in Virginia, I competed in the international speech contest with an speech entitled: 'The Power of Prayer'. I described the earthquakes (but not Elvia Maria's experience because it had not yet happened). I won the competition at club level, then lost at area level. My friend John Li , who was a member of the jury, said—'Marco your speech was the best, but I think that the judge docked points for your accent.'

I competed again in 2005 in Florida with the same speech, this time adding Elvia Maria's experiences. Again, I won at club level; and again, I lost at area level—though that may have been due to my exceeding the time limit. Luckily, I had already learnt the lesson of loss, and accepted it graciously. I concluded the speech by asking everyone to pray when they wake up, pray in the shower, pray in the car, pray for the sick, pray for the poor, and to pray with complete faith that God will hear your prayer and grant it. Once I had finished my speech, a lady approached me and said, 'Marco, I loved your speech because I pray as you requested. I pray in the shower, in the car, and God grants me what I ask.'

Lesson Three: Through thick and through thin you must pray, pray, pray. Pray to live a happy life filled with love. If you pray, God will give you everything.

CHAPTER FOUR: MY PARENTS' LIFE

My parents were born in San Mateo, a small town not far from Lima. Both were hired as primary school teachers. My father was tall and handsome; my mother, though short, thin, and very near-sighted, was always very cheerful and optimistic. It would appear that I inherited my father's innate tranquility and my mother's competitiveness and eyes. My grandmother Nicolasa told me that, once, she was walking to a farm with my mom and told her to avoid a puddle. Though my mother claimed she saw it, she walking right into it. My grandma then said, 'Chica, you're as blind as an owl,' (that never made sense to me as it is my understanding that owls see very well). I've used glasses since high-school, and as an older man I had a series of retina operations the eliminated any chance of becoming completely blind. I know that my eyesight isn't too bad as I can still hit that yellow ball in tennis. I inherited perseverance, ambition and love of study and work and a heart of sportsman who always liked to win from both of my parents. I can confidently say that I've always been a deep sleeper, so deep that I can sleep anywhere, even with an orchestra playing beside me, just like my dad, and usually quiet and docile. But, I am always aggressive, and ambitious bordering on arrogance, when making important decisions, I always made sure to choose the best option. For example, when I won the Fulbright scholarship to study in the United States, I asked:

"Which is the best Catholic University in the United States?
The answer came—
"The University of Notre Dame."
"Then, I am going to go to Notre Dame," I said firmly.
My father worked in the Cerro de Pasco Cooper
Corporation in Casaplace as an employee in the office of
public relations. In addition, he worked as the manager of
the local cinema. He would sell tickets, then operate the film
camera. It was the era of silent film, with only a piano
playing in the background. We lived in a house that
overlooked the village sport's pitch, where we played
soccer, and more importantly (and excitingly) bullfight's
occurred there. I loved playing soccer with my friends, and
one day I was chosen to be the goal keeper. I knew that my
mom had thin gloves, and I took them. After the game, I
returned home and tried to hide the dirty gloves behind my
back. But, with the uncanny accuracy of mother's intuition,
she guessed that I was hiding something. She confronted
me, and I had no choice but to show her the gloves. My
punishment was to wear one of my sister's dresses so that I
wouldn't go outside— and, as it was a Sunday afternoon,
there was a professional football game on. Luckily, our
house faced the field, and I opened a window to watch the
match. I remember, my dad had a toy referee whistle, and I
began to watch the game. I soon saw more than three
players fighting for the ball, and evidently my punishment
had not rid me of all mischief, for I blew the whistle— and
quickly closed the window. The players stopped, and
everyone was very confused. The referee continued the
game, and I repeated the joke several times. The players
were all very frustrated, if not downright furious, but I was
never discovered. As an employee of the office of Public
Relations, my dad had the responsibility to give licences to
businessmen who wanted to open shops in the town. One
day, a Japanese man entered my father's office and asked
to open a grocery store. My father gave him the necessary
paperwork and told him that once it had been completed
and checked, he would call him. A week later my dad called

the man and gave him the requested license, which was free of charge. The man hated in to my father money in the amount of 50 soles, which at that time was a lot of money, perhaps the equivalent to The man gave my father 50 soles, which at the time was equivalent to approximately $500 dollars. My dad tried to return the money, as it was free of charge, but the man insisted, saying it was for his help. Again, my dad protested, but the man said that he would be offended if his gift was not accepted. Reluctantly, my dad accepted it with many thanks to Mr Tamashiro. My dad's friend became the accountant of the Japanese man's shop, and saw in his books $50 soles for Mr Egoavil for the license. The friend reported the case to his superiors, and my dad's boss said: 'You charged $50 soles for a licence. That is dishonest and unacceptable. You are fired.' My dad stayed silent—there was nothing to say. Despite his honesty, he had done something that looked dishonest. My dad told us this story, so 'you learn that in life it is not enough to be honest, you must always seem honest as well.'.

Lesson Four: A lesson from my dad, to be honest you must seem honest.

My mom passed away in San Mateo at thirty five years of age. My dad put the three older children (Marina Antonieta, Milagro Angelica, and Marco Antonio) in the school: "Colegio Peruano de los Sagrados Corazones de Barranco". My aunt Carlota Suarez was the Principle. We boarded at the school along with other students. There was a German girl the same age as me who lived with her mother, and my aunt asked her mother to tutor us. The girl and I shared a room, played together, learned and were disciplined in the German style. My brother's Cesar Augusto and Carlos Magno stayed with my grandma Nicolasa in San Mateo, though Cesar soon joined us at school. The three Egoavil siblings, Milagro, Marco, and Cesar were unbeatable playing bata, a game similar to softball. Aunt Carlota liked to organize theatre shows for the students. Milagro was a born artist, she simply spouted poetry, and won the admiration of anyone who had the chance to see her in the shows. She recited 'La Carreta' and made the whole audience cry. As she spoke, she incorporated such emotion into her voice that everyone around her felt them, too. Afterwards, I saw my aunt silently crying by the piano.

 'Aunt Carlota, why are you crying,' I asked. She answered, 'Tomorrow, you are all going to live with your dad in Callao, and I am going to miss you terribly.'
My father had married Lady 'Gevita' Genoveva. My step-mother was a serious woman, and very strict with us children. She was also very religious, and I liked to go to mass with her on Sundays at 6:30am, at Bellavista Church. 'Bellavista' means beautiful sight in Spanish. As we lived in Vigil, we had to wake up at six in the morning to walk the eight blocks up the Hill Avenue to the Church. We would always kneels in front of the Sacred Heart of Jesus. Lady Gevita always gave something, but I didn't knew how much as she never gave me the coin to give to the collection.
I had my First Communion on the 8th of December 1939—the year in which my wife was born. In continuation, I've always been very religious; after my First Communion I woke up early to receive communion every first Friday of the month for ten consecutive years. I hope that Saint Peter has this well recorded. My dad was diagnosed with colon cancer and successfully operated, but he needed a bag by his side to have bowel movements. As a Professor of the School of Technology of the National University of Engineering, I applied and won a UNESCO Fellowship to study in England and the USA for six months, each. But, it was yet uncertain how long my dad was going to live, and I thought it unfair for my family to go far away. Surely I wasn't a good son if I went travelling when my dad could die in my absence? I consulted with several doctors, with priests, with teachers. All told me to travel. At the time we only had

Elvita and Beatriz, and we travelled to Wolverhampton in England where I would learn how to conduct courses of engineering at Wolverhampton Technical Teacher's College. The British Council of Lima had recommended I travel alone, and leave my wife and two young daughters at home, because finding a house to rent in Wolverhampton was notoriously difficult. But I knew at once I could never leave my family behind. I told them I wouldn't travel alone, and courteously thanked them for the recommendation. Days later, at the Lima international airport, I said goodbye to my extended family—and my dad. Hugging him, I felt the bag at his hip, and tried not to cry. Remaining calm, I embraced my family one by one. My Aunt Carlotta was last, and she said,

 'Goodbye, God will take care of you.' At those words I could no longer suppress my tears, and I began to cry profusely, my arms around her. I reluctantly relinquished the careful control of my emotions, exhausted from the effort, and let the tears fall freely. Perhaps, I cried for my dad who might not be there to welcome me home, which unfortunately became reality.

Upon arriving in London we went to our hotel where we stayed for three days, and explored the wonderful city. We were also introduced to the British Council, where they again told me I should not have brought my family and confirmed the difficulty of renting a flat. Slightly concerned now, we arrived in Wolverhampton and checked into our hotel. We bought a pot to heat milk for the girls, which we still have forty five years later. My wife loves it, and always uses it. At the time, Elvita was six and Beatriz five. Next day, I read the local newspaper, but did not see any advertisements for apartments. Still undeterred, I put a notice in the local post office that I was a Peruvian students sponsored by UNESCO with a wife and two daughters who wanted to rent an apartment for half a year. I soon received a call from a Mr Elsbury, who informed me that he had a house I could rent. After receiving the address, we immediately went to see it. The cottage came fully furnished

and was very stylish, it even had a modern television set.
The couple was to travel to Spain for six months, and
desperately needed to rent out their home. We all agreed
that it was a match made in heaven.

**Lesson Five: Do not spend your life separated form
your family from very long, it is to be enjoyed together.**

After we rented the house, I called the British Council and
told them, very respectfully of course, that I had found the
perfect house for us. I suppressed a laugh gleefully— I had
done the seemingly impossible. My training was comprised
of visiting factories, and within a week I went to Rugby to
work with the engineers of the Rolls Royce Co.. The visit
included a delicious lunch and drink. I told my young
English host that he could request the drink for me; he
ordered one scotch whiskey with lemonade for him, and
one for me. The glass was absolutely gigantic, and that
marked the beginning of my love affair with whiskey.
Whenever I have the chance, I order a whiskey with
lemonade and smile to think of my time in England.
We must not forget my family. Elvia called me every night,
and on the second night she told me, crying, that Beatriz
had tripped and hit her mouth against the corner of the
door. She had comforted her, washed her mouth, and
noticed that a tooth was hanging by a thread. Elvia knew
little English, so when she contacted a hospital they could
hardly understand what she was saying. Luckily, God
looked down on use and someone managed to surmise
what she was saying, and immediately sent an ambulance.
Despite the recent abundance of snow, they arrived quickly
and took them to the hospital, where they fixed Beatriz's
tooth. Understandably, my wife was under a considerable
amount of stress during this occurrence, and was worried
that I would be away. Luckily, I had talked with the landlord
of the inn, and she suggested my family travel to me, and
that she would arrange for another bed in my room. They
took the train, and I scheduled my visits to factories to be

able to greet them at the station. Elvia assured me that they would be absolutely fine. Next day, I was waiting at the station when the train rolled in right on time,
The passengers began to get off the train, I walked up and down to see if they had come. Almost all of the passengers had got off, and I still saw no sign of my family. Heart heavy, I assumed the worst and thought that they had missed the train. Then, far away, I saw Elvia and the girls getting off of the train in their winter coats and hats. I almost cried for joy, and ran to them.
 'Why were you so late?' I asked.
'The girls needed the toilet at the last minute!' came the reply, and we all laughed. Since that day, my wife has earned the reputation of being a very punctual traveller.

Lesson Six: A lesson from your Grandma Elvia, always be prepared for everything you do, nothing should intimidate you and always remind yourself that someone will be waiting at the station for you.

Once I had finished my training in England, we travelled to the United States, to the University of Illinois. We stopped in Chicago to visit my siblings, and had a delightful time. At the university, I attended all the lessons of a certain Professor Hull, who taught Design of Gas Turbines and Internal Combustion Engines. He was also developing research on turbulence in the combustion chambers of engines. We stayed in the special residence for married graduate students, a small two bedroom apartment. One weekend in March, my sister Marina, Milagro with her son Moisesitio, Aida and her husband and children, came to visit us. It was very cold; there was snow on the roofs. On Sunday, I woke up early and took a quick shower, then made breakfast. Suddenly, I heard a shout. Milagro told me that she was soaping her son when the hot water ran out— it was cold as ice. The apartment was, as stated, small, and the water heater too. I ran to the kitchen and heated a big pot of water for my nephew to finish his bath. I decided that, when I bought a house, I would put in a large heater. Always plan ahead for unforeseen circumstances; to generalise this idea, always have backup plan in life in case something goes wrong. My sister Marina called me the next week, and said in a strange voice that she was going to pay us a visit. Immediately, I thought of my dad, but desperately told myself not to worry. My sister greeted us, and made us sit down after many preambles.

'My dad died two days ago.' (We always used 'my' dad instead of ours, a way of talking which my children later inherited). Then, Marina looked at Elvia and told her her dad had died four days ago. At that, we both began to cry inconsolably. Although our children were to young to understand what had happened, they started sobbing, too. Through her tears, Elvita asked:

'Why are you crying, why am I crying?'

'Your grandfathers died.'

'Why did they have to die?' My wife couldn't speak through her tears, so I answered,

'God decided to take them and now they're both in Heaven, with Him.'

CHAPTER FIVE: HOW I LEARNT PUBLIC SPEAKING

As a student of Notre Dame, a friend once invited me to attend the meetings of South Ben Toastmasters Club. At first, I attended out of curiosity, because I was shy and wanted to learn how to speak in public properly; but it soon became a club of camaraderie. In addition to being naturally shy, I spoke English with a heavy accent, so I figured the club was perfect for me. I was not wrong; I was an active member of the club for fifteen years. During that time I acted as Secretary, Treasurer, VP of Public Relations, VP of Education, and President of the Club, sometimes holding each position for two consecutive years. After taking the Dale Carnegie speaking course, I founded the Lima Toastmasters Club. The club members were comprised of young executives, fellow engineers, and my good friend Carlos Vildozo, an architect. I was also Area Govern or in Hampton, VA, as a member of the NASA Langley Toastmasters Club.

All speakers can be split into to groups: natural speakers and learned speakers. First, natural speakers are those who are born with the innate ability to express their thoughts and emotions in words— they can express themselves easily, and talk tirelessly for hours. Such speakers include Presidents Abraham Lincoln, Ronald Reagan, William Clinton, and Barack Obama. Many of my friends are natural speakers, especially my friend Regina Spellman, whom I met at NASA Langley Research Centre. She joined the Toastmasters Club, and I was her tutor. She won first place in ten consecutive competitions during her first year at the club. In all of my fifteen years at the club, no one else ever accomplished that feat. Now, we return to the second group. The learned speakers are those who study in order to master the subtle art of talking. Of course, I belong to the second group. For me, I learned to lose my fear of speaking in public through the club, and am forever grateful. To explain the process of mastering speech, in the first stage of training (after two years as an active member) an amateur toastmaster can confidently deliver a speech. The second phase occurs in the the following two years, during which the speaker gains the ability to perform impromptu speeches—speeches not prepared in advance. Upon hearing the title of the speech, you can within seconds start talking, fluently and eloquently. When confronted with such a task, beginners often freeze, cry even, and sit down without saying a single word. I have, regrettably, witnessed many such instances. However, I am always amazed to see that within a year or two of that embarrassment their newfound confidence, and how much they have learned. The third stage of a learned toastmaster is learning to speak as though they were a natural speaker. They may be, at this point, VP of Education or President (as I was) and they then initiate their training as a teacher. They then help beginner toastmasters, and thus the cycle continues.

My career as a toastmaster was effectively ended when I realised I could no longer help the beginners in their noble endeavours. They named me as my friend Lisa Calloway's mentor. She was a cheerful, enthusiastic, young lady who took rather a long time to prepare speeches. After a year and a half of membership, she had delivered only five speeches. A very punctual member, she attended every meeting and knew all of the rules, methods, and formulas recommended for the development of speech. I assisted Lisa in her training to become a leader as she began to assume important positions (Toastmaster of the day, General Evaluator, Table Topics Master). The one problem

she had was that she did not enjoy preparing speeches. She started to miss meetings. So did I— and I realised I was not being helpful at all to her. I decided to retire from the Riverwalk Toastmasters Club. Therefore, I recommend to all of my eleven grandchildren and great-grandchild to focus on their speech, whether in a club as I did, or in college. Much preparation is needed in order to deliver a successful speech. I developed my own method, of which I am rather proud: I began by choosing the topic, which should be something from my own experience and one which I had the right to speak about. You must always write truthfully. Usually, these speeches lasted five minutes, which I checked during the writing of the speech. I would then rehearse in front of a mirror, and recorded it. Once satisfied, I asked my wife to be my audience. She would constructively criticise me, pointing out my weaknesses and strengths. Then, practice, practice, practice. In the car, at work, at home, I would practice. The day before the competition, I always knew the speech by heart— this technique often meant that I was the best speaker in the room. Sometimes, I would come home and happily announce 'I won first place!' Inevitably, my wife would ask how many speakers were present. Normally, there were two or three, but I often had to admit that I was the only one, so of course I won. Below, is my best speech from such a competition. The title is: It's incredible, I cannot believe it. One day, my daughter Veronica called her mother from New York, and said:
'Mom, FedEx (where she was working) has invited all of its employees to Hawaii, where they'll present the award to the best employee. I can take someone, do you want to come?' Ecstatically, Elvia answered,
'Of course!' The following week, a plane full of employees landed in Hawaii and took a small boat to the island of Maui. Veronica and her mom went to their room, then down to dinner. They told me that the sky was beautiful, a brilliant red streaked with shimmering golden rays. Just as they were finishing their food, the manager told them to turn on

their television sets— a hurricane was coming. Indeed, hurricane Iniki was going to hit Hawaii, and was currently headed straight for Maui. Everyone was advised to fill their bathtubs with water, take food from their fridges, and go to the basement with blankets and pillows. Veronica took her book (the Firm by John Grisham), and read all night. Suddenly, the lights went out— the hurricane was passing over the hotel. They slept at times, and when they did not sleep they would pray. Finally, they were told to go and review their rooms. All of the floors except for the fourth were completely flooded. Then, they went outside. All exclaimed how incredible it was, they couldn't believe it. Doors and windows were shattered, a big tree still with its roots was in the pool, underground cables were wrenched up, palm trees had fallen, and waves crashed on the shore at the beach. All of the employees assembled and it was announced that they would travel in a ship especially for them, and could only take a handbag each. They left discreetly, as to not alert the other guests. Elvia advised Veronica to bring her wallet and a pair of panties. After arriving in Hawaii, they were given the choice of taking a plane to Los Angeles that day or the next. Some decided to stay, including Veronica and her mom. They visited Pearl Harbour, and went shopping. A week after arriving home, Veronica called her mother to tell her that there was to be a meeting at Federal Express where the awards would be presented. The meeting opened by announcing the agenda— and the award ceremony was last on the itinerary. Miner awards were presented, and, finally, the President said: 'Now, it is time for the first prize, the best seller of the year is…' he described the records made, and said, 'The Best Employee of the Year 1988 for Federal Express Company, breaking all the sales records of the company is (he paused to create suspense)…Veronica Egoavil! Veronica please approach the podium".
The prize was a glass eagle with outstretched wings. Veronica and many other employees couldn't believe it. This wasn't to say she didn't deserve the prize, everyone

felt that she deserved it, and was very proud. This lesson of this story is for my grandchildren to aspire to be as successful as their Aunt (or mother) Veronica, and to always try their best. Of course, success is important, but not nearly so much as happiness. Veronica made her mother so happy by choosing to take her, and not a friend as some of her colleagues did. It was a wonderful experience for both of them, despite never even dreaming that a hurricane might have struck the trip. Always think of your parents first, and try to make them as happy as they make you.

Lesson Seven: a lesson from your Aunt Veronica, be the best at what you do, and be grateful to your mother too.

CHAPTER SIX: AGGRESSIVENESS AND SHYNESS

I was born shy, and as a young boy I was especially shy with women. But, though God gave me shyness in social situations, he gifted me with aggressiveness in sports and decisions throughout my life. My definition of aggressiveness, in this book, is striving for the best when making important decisions in your life. It is the absolute opposite of shyness. As previously touched upon, I first kicked a soccer ball when I was three; when I was four, I developed a fear of women. As a child, my cheeks were red as a Chilean apple, a trait which made my aunts quite literally eat my cheeks with kisses every time they saw me. Due to my shyness I think that I lost a platonic love of my life— I did not dare to even ask her name. The love was a seventeen year old fair-haired girl from Chucuito. Every day, Monday to Friday, she took the electric tram to the Commercial Academy. I lived at 270 Constitutions Street, and I too took the tram to go to university. On the first day of lessons my outfit including the beret worn by all of the freshmen. We all sat in chairs controlled by older students, who cut our hair until our heads looked like coconuts. One freshman was prepared, and pulled out his beret that he had bought beforehand. All of the 'cachimbos' (freshmen) were proud to be students at such a fine university. The fair-haired girl generally wore red dresses, and for that reason I christened her: 'the girl in red'. The girl in red always travelled with her green-eyed friend. Sometimes, she would knit on the tram, and I would take the opportunity to subtly draw an outline of her figure. Her hair was cut like Doris Day. I never tried to talk to her, and did not know her name, but the few times our eyes met it seemed to me that she liked me, perhaps not as much as I her, but still. During the summer, there were carnivals, and the girl in red went to a dance in the park dressed in white; her escort a nice young man very well dressed. Once, I was sitting on a bench when she walked by me, her dress flowing behind in resplendent white. She gave me a smile, and the sweet scent of her perfume wafted over. It was a happy moment for me. A second happy moment was when I entered the Matrix Church in Callao and saw the two friends, the girl in red and the green-eyed girl sitting in the third row near the main door of the church. I sat in the last row, and for some reason she turned around, noticing that I was there. I was wearing my shiny faux leather jacket that I had bought in New York. She whispered something to her friend, who also turned and saw me. I was happy to know that they were talking about me. But for what intent, you ask, do I describe these moments of platonic love to my grandchildren? In this lesson, I hope for them to learn the differences between shyness and aggressiveness, why did I never ask the girl in red her name? Why do I now, after all these years, have nothing to cherish but a nameless memory when I could have a friendship? The answer, in essence, is simple. I was shy. I was an introvert. I still am, to an extent. Being shy is to be afraid to publicly speak (which I am proud to have conquered), being aggressive is to make decisions without fear of anything. In public speaking I was shy by nature, for example in high school in Callao High School in the general meeting of all the students in the assembly room, the teacher asked all of the students who had gone on a trip to describe their visit to Trujillo. I had prepared a speech, and I knew it by heart, but when it was my turn I soon I felt a stab of panic and forgot everything. Another embarrassing experience in regards to public speaking was in my first year of engineering school. Professor Tudela, of Analytical

Geometry, called me to the blackboard to solve a problem. I began to solve the problem and then he asked me to explain what I was writing. I opened my mouth to talk, but nothing came out. By then, this was a commonplace occurrence, and he cracked a joke. Later, I will tell you more about my shyness and my agressiveness. If you are between eleven and twenty-six years old, no matter what country you're in, you could be, hypothetically, my grandchild. As your grandfather I advise you to read this book and to keep it as a reminder to further your education in your chosen career. All of the young boys and girls in Agrica, Asia, Australia, Europe, and North and South America ought to read this book in order to plan an education that will pinnacle in a Ph. D. It will be amazing not only for you, but also for your family who will be very proud of you. Throughout this journey, your family, friends, and teachers can help you in many small ways, but the real work is up to you. Always work hard. If you do, you will have made this world a better place. May I offer you my sincerest congratulations. Now, I would like to write especially for my granddaughter Veronica Gerdts. Veronica didn't take the initiative when it came to deciding about university. She finished high school, and when asked which career she would enter her reply was always: I am young, I am working now, I will decide later. Obviously, I'm a big fan of education, and I desperately tried to persuade her to go to college in a letter that I wrote:

Dear Veronica,
As you know, I am writing a book with life-lessons for my grandchildren. This is one of the lessons. The main reason I moved to the United States was so that my children could receive the best education in the world. I now wish to extend that aim to my grandchildren. You must go to university. God will help you, and we must pray. So please, please pray and ask God to help you to enter a university. You are astute, and have noticed that life is not easy at all. In fact, it is well described in the prayer: 'life is a valley of

tears'.I have cried many times in the many difficult moments of my life, and I would always pray, and that helped me to solve my problems. When I was your age, I lived in Callao and wanted desperately to study in the United States. I honestly hope that you seriously consider my propositions, and remember, I only ever want the best for you. I studied at the American School in Callao since the third grade— so I had classes in Spanish and English. In secondary school, I studied mathematics in Spanish; my teacher was Mr Labarte, a very old man who often fell asleep in lessons. Zoology, botany, and anatomy were taught in Spanish by Professor Galarza, a student studying medicine at the University of San Marcos. Physics and chemistry were taught in English by Mrs Wade, the wife of the principle who was a very pretty blonde lady, and who looked more like a movie star than a teacher. My teacher Mr James Carey, later principle, taught Ancient History, and English Grammar was dictated by Mr Shappel. My fifth year of high school came, and I attended a lecture by a Peruvian engineer who had studied in the United States. I was so enraptured and impressed by the lecture that I made up my mind that I would study in the United States. Immediately, I sent letters of application to American universities. To my utter delight, the University of Colorado accepted me as a student, and advised me about the expenses: tuition, room, board, books, etc. But, the cost was too high for my family. We were a large family, with three brothers, and three sisters. So I went to the American Embassy and asked what I could do to get a scholarship. After some tests and interviews they recommended I first consider a career in Lima, and then it would be far easier to obtain a specialised post-graduate scholarship in the US. Given that advice, I decided to study mechanical engineering at the National University of Engineering, but entering was not easy. I did a series of tests in arithmetic, algebra, geometry, trigonometry, physics, and chemistry. There were three-thousand applicants and only one-hundred spots. Hopeful, I took the exams— and finished three-hundredth. Tears were in my eyes as I read the results. When I got home and told my family about my failure, they understood my frustration and sympathised with me. But, after a week of sadness, I said to myself:

'Now I will study harder and be better prepared to enter the university next year.' Despite my plans, God decided that I would travel to the United States that same year.

One day in 1949, my dad came home from work and asked me if I wanted to go to the United States as a sailor in the merchant navy of Peru. The Peruvian Steamship company where my dad worked was hiring sailors to bring six vessels (that the Peruvian government had bought from the US) from Liberty in New York in Callao. Without much thinking, I said I would like to go. The First Engineer of the ship was Mr Juan Aristegui, and he happened to be my dad's friend. My name appeared on the list of sailors assigned to the engine room of the ship named Napo. Mr Aristegui interviewed me and explained that as a Wiper my duties were to keep the engine room neat and tidy, that the bronze had to shine and the walls had to be re-painted. I tell the entire story of my trip to the United States in a later chapter. We travelled by plane on the 25th of January 1949 to New York. After returning, I still tried to pursue a career in Mechanical Engineering. I monitored myself strictly, staying at home to study mathematics, physics, and chemistry; with the brilliant professor and exceptional engineer Roberto Heredia, who had a golden reputation throughout all of Peru. I again took the entrance exams for the University of National Engineering in March of 1950. I finished one-hundred and twenty-fifth. My score still wasn't enough to enter the university. I was devastated but not in tears when I told my family of my failure; they were again very comforting and understanding. I had the money from my work as a sailor, so I entered Pre-Engineering: a new section of the University that specifically prepared students for the tests. Clearly, this helped me enormously, as I tried again- undaunted- and finished twenty-fifth! We celebrated like we had won the lottery, and I thanked god for giving me the perseverance to continue my academic pursuits. My struggle to enter university taught me a very important life-lesson that I would like to pass down to my grandchildren. Life is not easy, there are many set-backs and failure is inevitable for everyone, but with determination and faith in God you can achieve your dreams. To persevere in the face of failure is to succeed. The first year of engineering school was hard for me. I studied every day, Saturdays and Sundays included. My only entertainment was going to the movies, I loved the musical films of Doris Day and Frank Sinatra- I even saw 'Tea for Two' five times. During my senior year, I started to go to parties. The intent of these parties was to meet girls, dance, and have fun with a few new friends for the future. My two best friends were Sergio Barba (who also studied Mechanical Engineering), and Carlos Vildozo (who studied architecture), may they rest in peace. Occasionally, we met up with another Mechanical student, Macario Rojas (RIP). I later went on to become the god-father (in the Baptismal Church) of his son, who was named Marco Antonio in my honour. We were not tall, handsome, Adonis' with sculpted muscles, but our academic status attracted girls. At the beginning of the gatherings, we would observe all of the girls around us, perhaps cautiously venturing to get a drink. I was still very shy. We would decide which girl we'd ask to dance. Of course, everyone wanted to dance with the most beautiful, smiling, red-lipped girls, but in my experience they are not always as nice as they look. Then, we would meet at the bar and ask each other who they were going to ask. We would avoid the question, and go and get a beer. After a few beers we were suddenly braver, and asked girls to dance- and they accepted. The girls danced well, like three Cinderella's, though she had not yet come. Sometimes I thought that once I got my Engineering diploma and a job I would marry, but I vowed, rather ironically, not to get married until obtaining a Masters degree in the United States. As soon as I got my first diploma I went to the US Embassy and completed the application requesting a scholarship for post-graduate study at a North American university. After two months of exams and interviews, they advised that I gain work experience in Peru in order to decide which course I would like to study. I talked with the Chairman of Mechanical Engineer Dr Tomas Unger whilst searching for a possible position. Coincidentally, the very same day I talked to him he had received a request from a company asking for a good graduate Mechanical Engineer. The position was perfect. Dr Unger wrote a letter of recommendation and I went to talk with the manager of the company. I met Mr Gonzalo Rosello, with whom began a beautiful professional relationship. After the interview, he offered me the job. He said that he liked my face and personality, and that he thought me honest. We then discussed salary, and he proposed 1,800 Peruvian soles. But my other classmates were receiving 2000 soles, and I thought that I ought to get the same. Finally, he relented and accepted my request. I went home a very happy engineer with a job. For five years I worked in the company, designing and fabricating mining equipment. We used non-metallic materials, such as cement. I was extremely lucky to work Gonzalo, because though he was an industrial engineer, he had a natural ability for solving Mechanical Engineering problems, especially in machine design- the field with which I was fascinated. Whilst working at Agregados Calcareos, I enjoyed my job so much that I often laughed when I was alone, with the pure joy of doing what I love. I worked all day at my drawing board, calculating the machine elements needed, then designing the dimensions of the machines, and then drawing the product with minute detail, so that it could later be easily manufactured and tested. I designed many machines, but typically I would do: grinding machines, hammer jaws, rotary machines, tumble mills, elevators, horizontal and vertical conveyors, cyclones to separate materials, limestone mills, and bag filters. My job included overseeing the manufacturing of my machines, followed by their complete installation (including the foundation and electrical components necessary to run them). Many times I had to modify them as I had made mistakes, or something hadn't turned out the way I had envisioned. Mistakes count towards experience, and experience is invaluable. Towards the end of my fifth year there, I went again to the American Embassy and requested a scholarship. After four months of tests and interviews I received a letter from the American Embassy that read:

Dear Mr Marco Egoavil:
We are pleased to inform that the government of the United States of America is granting you a Fulbright Scholarship and a Smith Mundt Scholarship to pursue post graduate studies in Mechanical Engineering at the University of Notre Dame, South Bend, Indiana.

I was overwhelmed with happiness, because I felt that my dreams had finally come true. They began when I attended a lecture at High School, then struggled through entrance exams for university, then working in a mining company, then applying for a scholarship, and finally, finally, after fourteen years those dreams came true. The scholarships generously covered all of my expenses, down to every last detail. the icing on top of the cake was when my boss Gonzalo offered that I receive half of my regular salary as I studied, not he condition that I return to work at Agragados after completing my studies. I agreed. Upon arriving at the University of Notre Dame, I stayed in the dormitories in the tower of Morrisey Hall. I went and bought clothes, warm for the winter, and an elegant lightweight trench coat. I returned to Peru two years later with a Master's Degree in Mechanical Engineering from the University of Notre Dame. I was now a man ready to get married. Exactly a year later, I married your grandmother Elvia in Cali, Colombia. It is described in more detail in a later chapter. In 1981, I received my diploma of doctor in Mechanical Engineering from Notre Dame. At my graduation, the guest speaker was President Ronald Reagan. Pat O'Brien, the actor, was also invited to the graduation, and President Reagan mentioned the famous phrase 'make one for the Gipper'. I would like my grand-daughter Veronica to know that because I went to university, I earned not only a degree but the respect of everyone I knew. Because I went to university, I learned how to solve problems and make good decisions. Because I went to university, I qualified to be a Professor of Engineering; at the end of my career I got a job in one of the most famous laboratories in the world, the NASA Langley Research Centre. You probably have plans for your life, but you alone have to decide which path to take, your friends and family can only help you make a decision. You are solely responsible for the roads you take during your life. We can all get God's help, all you have to do is ask. You simply say: 'God, help me to go to College," and pray the Our Father. Pray during difficult times. I myself recommend praying every day. Pray in everything you do, in the shower, in the car on the way to work. Pray that you get into a university, that your friends are alright and your family healthy. I have had many positive experiences concerning the power of prayer. I am sure that you have ore than enough intelligence, and that you will find a career you love and live to be very happy working. God blessed you with the best mom in the world. Think, and tell me truly if college is no the best thing for you. Today you are young and pretty, you have your whole life ahead of you. Your future is in your hands. You are always with me, in my thoughts and prayers, for I pray that God helps you in your life. Your grandmother Elvia and I love you very much. May God bless you always.

From your Abuelo Marco

I sent that letter to my grand-daughter Veronica in 2010. I have not received a reply to that letter yet. I do not know if she even finished reading it, and she hasn't gone to college. Her brother Grant graduated High School this year, and the above letter is for all of my grandchildren. As I have previously mentioned, to win in sports you must have a plan for the game. A such, to succeed in life you must be prepared, and the best preparation is university. I believe that everyone should go to college, and it was my Aunt Carlota who taught me these ideas. I hope that all of my grandchildren go to university. I know that many of them are clever enough to study for a master's degree and then a doctorate. We have a family reunion every year in Connecticut and I felt immensely overjoyed when my granddaughter Ariana informed me: 'Abuelo, when I finish high school in four years, I will go to Oxford University to study English Literature and I will try get my Masters and my Doctorate.' To my ears, that was like the music of heaven, for one of my grand-daughters already planned to follow the path I had chosen. My ambitions for post-graduate studies, my perseverance in obtaining a scholarship, and ultimately achieving my goals were all with God's help. I am more than qualified to advise very high-school student to go to university, and then aspire to do post-graduate studies. My Aunt Carlota taught me that life-lesson, who studied French for her doctorate. As a child, she would ask me to test her on conjugate verbs. We both got out doctorates at about fifty years of age, which shows that you are never to old to go to school. In continuation of this theme, I'd like to mention my farewell party when I retired from NASA. In part of my thank you speech I said: 'I'd like to give advice to two of my friends and co-workers, who both have a Masters Degree in Mechanical Engineering, are married, and have several children. Chris Mourning and Jon Thompson, never think you are too old to return to school and get a doctorate, albeit it will not be easy with a wife and children, but from personal experience I can tell you, yes you can do it, yes you can go back to the university".

All of the lessons that I learned in the above, starting with the letter to Veronica and ending with advice to my friends can be summarised as follows:

Lesson 8: each one of you do whatever you want to do as long as you have defined aspirations and the perseverance to succeed.

Though I was shy by nature and with the ladies, I was aggressive in other aspects. Perhaps sports made me so; at school I competed in track, basketball, soccer, volleyball- I participated in every sport my school offered. We had an excellent teacher who organized matches all throughout the year. In West Palm Beach I played tennis every day and often played tournaments with neighboring communities. I was named Captain, and impressed upon the team that the most important thing was to win. Some disagreed, and said they should have fun. I maintained my position, and said that we have more fun if we win, so we should always aim to win. In 2009, as Captain of the level 9 tennis team of RiverWalk we got the first place in two tournaments: the '2009 West Palm Beach Senior Tennis Winter League' and the 'Fall 2009 Palm Beach Tennis League'. Another moment in which I showed aggressiveness was when I decided to move to the US with my family. At the time, I was Principle Professor of the Ricardo Palma University, and Director of the Academic Programme of Mechanical Engineering and the Head of the Department of Technology. My salary was high, seeing as I performed all three positions efficiently. The position was called Professor at Exclusive Dedication. A false rumour was circulated at the university, that I wanted to be Rector of the University. This was far from the truth, as it was more of a political and not academic position. I have never been interested in politics, and never attended the political meetings that my friends invited me too. A few years later, my friends Jorge Ratto and Abel Salinas, both engineers, concentrated on politics and reached high positions within the Peruvian government. Abel was a candidate for the presidency of Peru. But now, writing this, I received the sad news that my friend had died after a battle with cancer, may he rest in peace. Peru went through an uncertain time where the government leaned towards the left, and it seemed we were becoming a communist country. Universities were controlled by the National Board Education of Peru, who controlled all new ideas not only at a university level but also primary and secondary schools, and private schools. One day, I learnt that the Catholic School Real Felipe where my daughters attended, would be visited by members of the National Board. I went to observe them, and heard them say that the government would control their education. There were to be many radical changes, and it was insinuated that the country would become communist. It was then that I decided to emigrate the United States. Another factor influencing my decision was that at Ricardo Palma a big sign was painted onto the walls that read: EGOAVIL OUT. After that, I needed no further convincing. Next day I looked for a notary to draw up my resignation. My plan was to go to the US to get my PhD., but it was already August, and classes started in September. When I reached the lawyer's office, I began to doubt myself. I prayed to God to help me with my decision. I immediately felt calm, and sure in my decision. I entered the office. Thank God everything went well. I wrote a letter to Dr. K. T. Yang, Professor of the University of Notre Dame, who had been my counsellor before and requested admission to Notre Dame to pursue my doctorate. He immediately sent me all the papers I needed to get a student visa. I went to the American Embassy to request a visa, but I also was requesting a visa for my wife and four children. I was a little nervous because they could have denied us the visas. But the next week I received a call from a secretary who said that I could go and pick up the official papers. The embassy felt that our family would make good US citizens. The Peruvian government, represents by the National Board, did not learn of my departure. Or, on the contrary, they were happy that I left the country.

How I Emigated to the United States (subtitle under 'Aggressiveness and Shyness):

On the first of September in 1972, my wife, my four children and I arrived in Chicago. We stayed with my sisters for a few days, and then went to South Bend. We stayed with friends until the apartment for married students called: the Village of Notre Dame, was ready. After that briefly nomadic period of life, we were finally settled in an apartment of two bedrooms. The three girls shared a room and slept in bunk beds, while three-year old Marco slept in a cot in our room. Moving my family was not easy, we had to sell our house, the furniture, and the car. I was also leaving my work, and saying goodbye to family and friends, all without knowing exactly how this new adventure was going to go. But we had God's help through prayer, and we knew that we were going to live in a land of opportunity, a country with the best universities in the world. In reality, I moved to the US so that my children could receive the best education the world has to offer. I can say that I completed that goal: Elvia Angelica graduated from Notre Dame, Beatriz studied at Florida Atlantic University, Veronica has the Bachelor and Master of Business Administration from Georgetown and New York university respectively, and Marco Antonio has a Bachelor of Business Administration from Georgetown, Master's degree from New York University and he also graduated with a law degree from the University of Minnesota.

I have persevered and been aggressive when making decisions, and I would like to give this advice to my grandchildren:

Lesson 9. To succeed in life you must study hard in school and always gets good grades, record in your mind that it is essential that you should pursue a career in college and even study a master's degree and then a doctorate.

CHAPTER SEVEN: HOW I MARRIED A COLOMBIAN GIRL

The girl in red was not to be, God had a different girl in mind for me. When I returned to Peru I wanted to get married right away. Notre Dame extended my scholarship for an
additional semester in order to complete my master's studies. I decided to live in the city of South Bend instead of the dormitories of the university, so I started to look for a flat. A Colombian student approached me, as I read the bulletin board on housing, and said:

'If you're looking for an apartment, I have one. I need a roommate to help pay rent.' He very talkative, and told me about himself. I found myself liking him, and agreed to take the apartment with him. He was studying for his doctorate in literature, as my granddaughter hopes to do, and became an expert in the life of Ruben Dario. He was known as the Colombian who knew more about Ruben Dario than the people of Nicaragua. He taught at the university of Cali. One day I told Publio that I would like to meet intelligent and beautiful girls with the intention of marriage. I asked him if he knew anyone. Publio gave me the name of his cousin Elvia Duque, and I wrote to her immediately. I planned to visit my brother Carlos where he studied Veterinary Medicine, then visit my friend Horacio Pena in Nicaragua. Much to my amusement, he told me that all young people in

Cuba aspire to be musicians, and that all young people in Nicaragua aspire to be poets. The greeting among boys in Managua was: good day, poet. I did not meet any interesting girls in Mexico, nor Managua. I went to Panama and spent three days sightseeing, but still saw no girls. Then I travelled to Cali, Colombia, and Elvia Duque was waiting for me at the airport, as we had agreed by letter. When I got off the plane her sister Alicia met me, and lead me to Elvia.

We entered a large room where my future wife was sitting in a chair. We shook hands and exchanged pleasantries, she enquired about my trip. We went to my hotel in a cab, and I took the opportunity to look at her. She was slightly taller than me and had blonde hair. She was wearing a magenta sweater that showed her sexy bare shoulders, and a white skirt with revealed perfect legs, neither skinny nor fat. We bid farewell until the next day, when we had dinner at her brother's house. It was a simple meal, but very formal, and no opportune moments for romance. After the two-day visit, we parted with the promise to write. Then I left for Lima. Thus began a faithful and honest correspondence. I received, without fail, a letter every week. The letter always arrived in the morning, and when I came home at noon for lunch I would ask if it had arrived yet. Usually, nobody knew, but sometimes they would hide it to tease me. My brother-in-law Reynaldo always played the joker, and derived especial pleasure from this activity. We would play hot and cold until I found the letter, and everybody laughed at my joy upon its discovery. At the end of the year, in November, I wrote a letter that told her of my love and a proposal of marriage. She suggested that I travel to Cali to meet her parents and decide our future together. I asked for ten days of vacation from work during Christmas.I went once again to Cali on the twenty second of December, and Elvia greeted me. After breakfast the next day I went with Elvia and her sister Alicia to see the city. We had a traditional Columbian lunch and Alicia tactfully left us alone to talk. We walked along a river path and sat down on a bench. I spoke of how every single word I wrote was true. I told her I intended to ask for her hand in marriage from her dad, and that I loved her and wanted to make her happy. Being the arrogant young man I was, I thought that she would say yes, I love you too, let us marry. Instead she told me that her dad would come in a few days, and that we should wait for him to make a decision. I agreed to wait, and we talked for a bit more whilst walking through the city. We went by a movie theatre where a German musical was playing. I suggested that we enter, and she agreed. The theatre was half-empty, and we sat in the last row. Slowly, I took her hand, put my arm around her shoulder, hugged her, and finally kissed her. That was the yes I was expecting. Then we left, as it was getting late, and I dropped her off at home. I counted out my money and went to a jewellery store and bought a diamond engagement ring. I had paid the initial deposit upon ordering the ring, but I needed now to pay the full payment. I sent a message to my soon to be sister-in-law (with whom I had left my savings) and asked her to send me the money, adding in the message how wonderful Elvia was. That was on the twenty-third of December, and I prayed with all of my heart that it arrived before Christmas. Next day, I went to the Ermita Church and prayed that 1. the money the arrives on time, and 2. Elvia's dad gives me his blessing for his daughter's hand in marriage. Later that day, Alicia tried to persuade me to let Elvia go to university to study nursing. Rubelia had helped Elvia send all of the paper work for a scholarship at the university of Medellin, which had been approved. Alicia advised me to wait a year, and then get married. But I was worried that Elvia would meet a different boy. I was determined not to leave Cali without having asked her father for her hand. At noon, I went to the bank to check if the money had arrived, but the clerk there had nothing for me. As I left the building, I suddenly felt the ground shaking. It was an earthquake. I rushed to Elvia's house to see if everything was alright. Thank goodness

they were, and Elvia even greeted me with good news. She said:
'Tomorrow, my father and I are going to the bullfight, you can come too.'
I collected the money from the bank and went straight to the jewelry store to collect the ring. Early on the twenty-fifth of December I went to Elvia's house, where I first met Don Jesus. He was a tall gentleman whose large stature, unsurprisingly, intimidated a small fellow like me. He looked me up and down, and said:
'Are you ready to go to the bull fight?'

'Yes sir!' I answered eagerly. It seemed to me as though he had been waiting for me. We arrived at the stadium where an enthusiastic throng of people were getting their seats. We sat in this order: Don Jesus, Alicia, Elvia, and then me. Sometimes, when the bullfighter had a narrow escape or the bull came close to us, I bumped into Elvia, or she clasped my arm. We had a tremendous amount of fun. Upon leaving the bullring, Elvia told me that she had talked to her dad, and that tomorrow I would have lunch with him and her brother Gustavo. I could ask for her hand then. That was music to my ears. Overcome, I immediately pulled out the engagement ring from my pocket and gave it to her, entrusting it to her care for the rest of her life.
The next day, I met the men for lunch. My shyness once again dominated me, and I didn't know what to say. After several awkward silences, I made up my mind and said:
'Don Jesus, you know that I want to marry your daughter Elvia. I am a Mechanical Engineer with a Master's degree from the United States, and a stable job at mining company in Lima. In addition, I am a Professor who teaches mechanical engineering courses part-time at the National Engineering University of Peru. With my colleagues, I have created a company called Studies and Executions which develops engineering projects in Lima. Finally, I am a devout Catholic, and wish to marry Elvia in a ceremony in a Church.' Don Jesus looked at me, and asked:

"Does Elvia want to marry you too?' I replied that I was sure she loved me as much as I loved her, and that she had agreed to marry me. I was very relieved and glad to hear Don Jesus say:
'If that is so, I give you my blessing. Let me know when you will marry.'

On the eight of March, 1962, my aunt Carlota and I arrived at Cali (my father couldn't go). We stayed again at the Europa Hotel. The day before the wedding all of our friends and family, and even the priest, gathered for a meal. There was a delicious dinner and champagne. Gustavo told jokes about the day he got married, and everyone was happy.

Then, it was time for me to go to confession with the priest. I was slightly surprised, as I hadn't expected that, but I didn't mind at all. I went with the priest to a quiet room where I talked honestly and without reservation. I received Absolution. Next morning, I woke up at five, as I had to arrive at the church at six-thirty. My aunt and I took a taxi there. during the journey, she tried to tell me something, but couldn't find the words.

'Today is a big day for you. Life is hard…but I hope that you and your wife will be happy.'

It was still dark when we arrived at the church. A few minutes later, Elvia arrived. She wore a white dress and very little make-up. I raised my head to the heavens and thanked God for giving me a beautiful wife. We entered the church promptly at six thirty am., accompanied by Don Jesus, Dona Lola, Gustavo, Alicia, Maruja, and my aunt Carlota. The Father carried out the ceremony, and towards the end I hoped that he would say 'you may kiss the bride', but, regretfully, he didn't. Afterwards, we all headed to Gustavo's house for a large breakfast, including a wedding cake. At eleven, we went to Cali and signed papers for a civil marriage ceremony. At noon, we travelled to Miami for our honeymoon of three days, then another three days in Chicago where my siblings met my new wife, my 'esposita' as I loved to call her. In regards to marriage, I wish for my grandchildren to learn that:

1.   When you marry, trust your intuition, heart, and God.
2.   Get to know your fiancé(e) well, know their family, their likes and dislikes.
3.   Moments of joy are doubled when you marry- and so are the moments of difficulty and sadness. Perhaps your grandmother Elvia took greater risks than I when deciding to marry, but as I say above, trust your intuition and heart and she and I entrusted to God the union of our destinations. God heard us and looked after us, as much as 50 years and counting, as in March 10, 2012, we fulfill our Golden Anniversary.

Lesson 10. To marry trust your intuition, heart and God. Meet the family of the groom or bride. The moments of happiness in dating are duplicated in marriage. Moments of arguments and fights quadruple in marriage. Pray that God will help you when deciding to marry.

CHAPTER EIGHT: MY SISTERS AND BROTHERS

It is difficult to define precisely how many siblings I have, because my dad remarried after many years of widowhood. My step-mother was a fine lady named Genoveva, whom us children called Mrs Gevita, and I consider her children my brothers and sisters because we grew up together. My elder (step-) sister Alicia was a helpful and humorous girl who, like my sister Marina, never married. The Spanish saying 'marriage and mortice, from heaven comes' was especially true for them. I had six 'full' siblings: Marina Antonieta (R.I.P), Milagro Angelica, Efraim Esteban (R.I.P), Aida Petronila, Cesar Agosto, and Carlos Magno Pompeyo (R.I.P); and I had three step-siblings: Alicia, Alfonso, and Reynaldo. The more astute of my readers may have noticed that several of our names have historical origins- namely myself and my brothers Cesar and Carlos. They were given by my uncle Manuel Jesus Suarez, Professor of History at secondary schools in Lima. When my brother Carlos Magno Pompeyo was old enough, he made up his mind to officially change his name to Carlos Magno, thus simplifying it. The six eldest brothers finished their secondary education at Callao High School. The three girls finished secondary commercial- that is, they would get jobs as bilingual secretaries right after they graduated. In my class, ten boys signed up to study regular secondary school at Callao. Our diploma allowed us to continue studying at university. My youngest brother Carlos was the only one who did not study at Callao High School; he continued technical studies at the General Polytechnic of Lima, where he received the title of Electrical Technician. Carlos, looking for new and better prospects, emigrated to Mexico along with the economic and moral support of our elder sister Marina Antonieta, where he studied veterinary medicine and graduated as a veterinary doctor specializing in cattle. He got a job as a professor at the University of Chihuahua, where he taught and helped farmers to raise cows. In short, all of the Egoavil brothers emigrated from Peru to the

United States bar Efraim (who stayed in Callao because he felt an aversion to the 'gringo's' country) and Carlos (who emigrated to Mexico). Years later, Efraim changed his mind and settled in Washington DC.

Marina Antonieta

After graduating from Callao High School, my sister Marina obtained a job as Bilingual Secretary at various companies including Columbia Pictures of Lima (a film districutor) where she got free movie tickets. The whole family enjoyed those tickets. Then, Marina got a boyfriend who was of oriental heritage. To date such a man was a sin according to my dad, and he was clear from the beginning that he completely opposed Marina's relationship with him. My dad was the son of a Spanish gentleman, who had indoctrinated in him a feeling of hate towards black and Chinese people. He tried to teach the same to us, saying:

'You must improve your race when you marry.' This distorted racist concept continued in his view that we should never marry a black or Chinese person. But times have changed and I recognize now my father's prejudice, and advise my grandchildren to trust their heart and God. As previously mentioned, Marina never married, but in a way she was the mother of Cesar, Carlos, and myself. Marina was the foundation of the Egoavil brothers, and we would have crumbled without her. Marina had Alzheimer's and died in Celaya, Mexico.

Milagro Angelica

Milagro Angelica was of a cheerful nature, very like my mother my aunts told me. She was an excellent athlete- as you know, we were unbeatable in Bata as children. However she stood out most as a histrionic artist. In addition, she showed much talent for theatrical comedies, which were performed at the Barranco school. There was not a dry eye in the house when she recited the poem 'La Carreta'. She herself cried whilst reading. She finished high school, and us siblings at home still did not know whether she had a boyfriend, until one day, as I was walking in Lima along the Paseo Colon, I saw Milagro talking animatedly with a young man. As I got closer, I saw that the man had very dark hair and though his skin was not necessarily dark, Milagro looked like a ghost next to him. Surprised to see me, she introduced me to the man. We made small talk, and Milagro soon pulled him away, eager to get away from her annoying younger brother. Taking care that the man did not notice, she whispered to me under her breath: do not tell anyone. I did not tell anyone except for my elder sister Marina, who thought nothing of it. The occurrence was soon forgotten in our minds. Milagro, or Milos as we always called her, immigrated to the United States and settled in Evanston with my sister Aida who had settled there two years prior. For a while, they lived at the YWCA in Evanston and later moved to a house, searching for the American Dream. They become friends with the Asturrizaga's family, who were also from Peru. Milos caught the eye of Moises Asturrizaga, and it is suffice to say that he did not go unnoticed by her, either. Moises was a tall and sturdy man, very talkative, and was the owner, manager and cook of a Peruvian restaurant called 'El Piqueo' in suburban Chicago. Not long after they met, Milagro and Moises married. Their family grew when little Moises was born. The baby was not only named after his father, he took after him in his tall and robust frame. Little Moises became an athlete at High School and was an extremely good football player. But, and in life there are always buts, Moisesito had a strange illness similar to epilepsy. Some said it was because of the head blows from playing football. To the dismay of the whole family and his girlfriend, he passed away much too young at the age of 21 years old in 1990. During the funeral, it was time to close the coffin, and the gentleman in charge was directing people out of the room.   'Chispitas,' I called (my pet name for her), 'we have to go.' Crying profusely, she said: 'Yes- I know, I know. Just let me say my last goodbye to my baby Moisesito- let me pray and say farewell.' Silently, she prayed. Milos turned to go and walked towards the door, when suddenly she ran back to the coffin and cried and prayed again. This cycle repeated several times, until two gentleman escorted her out of the room. My brother Cesar, who was responsible for the order of the cars, told me that the two women whom Moises had loved in his life- his mother and girlfriend- would ride in the first car. We were to follow in the second car. Moises senior was 250 pounds, suffered from diabetes, high cholesterol, and high blood pressure. When asked about his cholesterol levels, he always replied that it was very low. When pressed for a precise figure, he would say: very low, only 300. Moises was a cook and ran a restaurant as previously mentioned, while it had moments of success it also had moments of desperation when no customers whatsoever frequented his restaurant. Moises was always an optimistic man. When we visited him in Chicago he always described his ideas of new original dishes, invented by him. Unfortunately, he did not take care of himself; it was considered nothing out of the usual for him to buy a gallon of ice cream and consume the entire thing in one sitting. The entire family suffered beyond words when Moises died of a heart attack in his bathroom. Moises was buried in the same cemetery as his son, Moisesito, and they were very near each other. Milos was wont to say how stupid she was for having only one child- it was true that one was like none. She regretted that, and it had rendered her all alone, a childless widow. This lesson is from your Tia Milagro. When you choose to have children, ask God to gift you with at least two children.

Lesson Eleven: Lesson from your Aunt Milagro: "When it's time to have children, do not have only one, ask God to have at least two".

Efraim Esteban

My older brother Efraim Esteban, whom we called Fayo, attended the same school as me throughout high school. In our senior year, that is, Fifth Year Secondary, we both wanted to study engineering. Efraim wanted to be a mechanical engineer, and I a mechanical engineer. Really, my calling was to be a pilot, but I encountered two problems, a pilot had to: be 5' 10" tall and have 20/20 vision. I, who had inherited my mother's short stature (I was 5' 3") and weak eyesight, was clearly not destined to become a pilot. I dreamt that perhaps, someday, I would design the engine of an airplane, so I chose to study mechanical engineering. My wish was fulfilled; at the end of my career I went to work at the NASA Langley Research Centre to design components of jet planes, specifically the combustion chamber of the aircrafts. I worked for NASA for 13 years, and loved every minute. Ultimately, Efraim changed his mind and decided that he wanted to be a doctor of medicine. Having finished his studies at the National University of San Marcos, he began his career, very pleased with his progress. All was well, until a friend took him to the racecourse San Felipe in Lima to watch a horse race. That was the beginning of the end for my brother Efraim. He was so enraptured with the races that he decided to end his career as doctor. Then, he got a job as a secretary at the American Embassy, and married a divorced lady who had already two children. My relationship with Efraim was rocky at best. We constantly competed; I recall that, when I was about twelve years old, we fought like wild animals. My brother Cesar was screaming,

'Marco, hit him, hit him harder!' Efraim was a slightly taller than me, but I was more muscular and he took the brunt of the fight. When my Dad came home from work the Lady Gevita told him about the fight, and he noted that Cesar encouraged me to hit Fayo hard. To our utter surprise, instead of punishing Efraim and I, my dad called Cesar and locked him in his room. We could all hear the belt lashes that Cesar received. Reynaldo, the eldest son of Lady

Gevita, proclaimed loudly that I and Efraim ought to be punished, not Cesar. Secretly, we all agreed. I see now that my dad was merely discouraging Cesar in his egging on of us. Rather philosophically, I often find myself wondering: why do brothers fight? why do parents use corporeal punishment on their children? I have no clear recollection of my kids fighting, nor how I punished them. My youngest daughter Veronica tells me that she and her younger brother Marco always fought. According to her, their mom would poke Marco with a broom to punish him. My grand-children often fight, but never with the severe consequences that resulted due to my and Efraim's fight. It left its mark. Years went by where we exchanged no words, not even when he came to live in the USA. Burdened by several ailments, including diabetes, high cholesterol and blood pressure, Efraim died (may he rest in peace) in Washington DC in 2003. I was told of his death three days after. Every time I think of him, I send a prayer for the soul of my elder brother Efraim.

Aida Petronila
Aida did not like her middle name 'Petronila', and she would complain whenever we called her by the pet name 'Petita'. Quite recently, I asked her why she disliked the name so. She replied,   'I know not why, but that name has always seemed so horrible to me.' Aida, whom we called Gringa because her skin was the whitest out of us siblings, worked at the US Embassy in Lima as a bilingual secretary. One day, she was invited to a party for employees at the embassy. My dad permitted her to attend on the condition that Efraim accompany her. Alas, Efraim had an infection in his nose and did not want to go to the party. My dad then asked me to accompany my sister, and I happily consented. A coworker of Aida's named Eduardo came to pick us up in his car. A chatty American guy kept patting Aida's knees, and Eduardo jokingly told him to keep his arms in front of him. We all laughed. Soon after, we arrived at the party, which was in a private house in San Isidro, and waiters and

waitresses offered us drinks. I took a glass of gin, and sipped it thoughtlessly. Despite its sweet and bitter taste, I suspected not that it contained alcohol, and accepted a second. I was an eighteen year old young man who had never before drunk liquor, and at about the eighth gin a terrible headache came upon me. I threw up and passed out on the sofa. I can't remember how we got home but someone must have put me in my bed, and I slept until noon the next day. When I tried to get up, the room spun uncomfortably. My headache was unbearable. I vomited the whole day and ate nothing. A vowed to never drink gin again, a vow I have not broken in my eighty-eight years of life. I suspect that if I ever do, for some reason, have a gin again, that my liver will die of PTSD. I recommend to all of my grandchildren that they be very careful with liquor, when they come of age, of course.

Lesson Twelve: when drinking liquor and eating fish you must be very careful. Be sure to never drink an excess of liquor.

Aida emigrated to the US and initially got a job in Lockport, Illinois near the University of Joliet where my brother Cesar was studying Chemical Engineering. Later, Aida moved to Chicago and lived in the YWCA with Milagro; when Marina moved to Chicago they rented an apartment together. The three sisters and their friend Erika shared the small apartment in Evanston. Marina worked at Sears, Milagro worked at Abbott Laboratories, and Aida worked at another pharmaceutical company. Aida met an American man named Jimmy who was very cheeky and mischievous, and, clearly charmed, she became his girlfriend. All of the Egoavils along with some friends went to celebrate Christmas in a restaurant in downtown Chicago. After enjoying the food and Jimmy's funny antics, we left. With a flourish, Jimmy produced the restaurant's menu, measuring 14" by 18". The menu was framed and became a prized possession in the sisters' house. Unfortunately, Aida's romance with Jimmy did not propser. She called me one day and said that she was travelling to San Francisco to visit Jimmy's friend Eduardo Arana who worked there. It was later revealed that Aida was going to San Francisco to marry said Eduardo Arana. They married in 1961, Elvia and I married in 1962, and Milagro and Moses several months after us. Two years later, in Virginia, Aida had a son whom they named Eduardito.

<u>Cesar Augusto</u>
Cesar Agosto was yet another athlete in the family. As you know, Milos, Cesar, and I won all of the bata matches at our school in Barranco. Cesar played football as a lefty, and his nifty left-footed kick scored us many a goal. When Cesar was in high school, his career aspirations fluctuated constantly, often in accordance with the latest film he had seen.

When we saw Clyde Beaty Lion Tamer he immediately stated his desire to become a professional lion tamer. When we read about poverty in Africa he wanted to become a missionary; he would go to Africa as a Catholic priest to help spread the Christian religion. Cesar followed my in my footsteps to become a sailor. He set sail on the Merchant Marine of Peru and travelled along the Pacific coast. From Central America he bought a parrot that was eventually entrusted to Mrs Emilia (sister of Lady Gevita). Defying all of the stigma that came with interracial marriages, Mrs Emilia married a Mr Ruiz, who was of African descent and owner of a bokstore in Colville, Callao, located in the commercial district in Constitution Street. Years later, my dad bought the building of the library, which consisted of three floor, and we all moved ther. Mr Ruiz was an excellent businessman— he was also the owner of four houses situated throughout the city of Callao. Mrs. Emilia gave birth to a dark-haired boy whom they named Armando, nicknamed affectionately 'Maño'. When Maño's friends saw him in the street they would shout: 'Maño, mojon de tu tamano,' which means Maño, landmark of your size. Maño Maño was my 'primo politico', a Spanish phrase that neatly fit our situation. Unfortunately, the term does not translate well into English, the best description is that he was my cousin, but not of my blood. Regarding sports, Maño was always the most awkward player on the field. If he ran the 50-metre sprint he would fall at the very least three times before reaching the goal. Whilst playing football, he never approached the ball, nor did anyone ever pass it to him. And now, back to Cesar. When Cesar finished high school, he was accepted into the University of Lockport, Illinois to study chemical engineering. The only reason he was able to go to that university was because of the moral and financial support from my sister Marina. When he finished his career he got a job in the candy factory Tohuy. It was his job to taste the final products, the envy of all children, though it weakened his body— especially his stomach. Consultations with doctors revealed that the candy had abnormal side effects. The doctors recommended that Cesar change his job right away. The factory removed Cesar from testing candies and, pretty soon, the stomach pains and other minor ailments had all but disappeared. At a Christmas part of Abbott Laboratories (where you'll recall Milagro worked) Cesar met a pretty lady with so much make up that she closely resembled a doll. Cesar told me that it was love at first sight, and the following year he married the lady, whose name was Elisa Williamson. The bride was the daughter of a Mexican lady and an English gentleman. Elisa and Cesar had two sons, Cesar Agosto who studied medicine, and Carlos Roberto. Today, Dr Cesar Agosto is a well known and prominent doctor of heart surgery based in Atlanta, and is married to another doctor who specialized in the heart. Unfortunately, Carlos Roberto was diagnosed with Diabetes Type One at birth, a condition that affected his whole life. He attended the University of Illinois at Urbana-Champaign. Carlos currently works as a manager at Costco in Chicago, and has not married. On a vacation, Cesar and Elisa travelled to Mazatlán, Mexico, the city where Elisa was born. Due to the climate, the cheap cost of living, the utter tranquility, and the welcoming character of Mexicans, Cesar persuaded Elisa to move to Mexico. They would spend the rest of their lives there. In 2004, Cesar decided to retire from work. Determined to settle in Mexico, he researched the best cities to live in. San Miguel de Allende was a beautiful place where many retired Americans lived. Cesar went to Allende and bought a four bedroom house with a large garden, and the following year Elisa retired from her job and went to live in Mexico with her husband. For mysterious reasons yet unknown, Cesar and Elisa separated and lived their lives apart. They are not divorced, nor have they married someone else. Of course, they visit their children Dr Cesar Egoavil in Atlanta and Carlos Egoavil in Chicago, but they go separately. My older sister Marina was diagnosed with Alzheimer's in 1992. She then led an almost normal life for about a decade. Marina had her own home in North Chicago when Cesar sold his house and bought a house near his work, taking Marina to live with him and his dog Rex, who was of the same bred as Rin Tin Tin. Then Cesar retired from his job at Tohui and bought the house in Mexico as mentioned above. Finally, Marina and Cesar settled in Celaya, a village 50 kilometers from Allende. The time came when Marina needed constant care, and Cesar decided to place Marina in an institution for the elderly run by Catholic nuns. In 1998, Milagro and I decided to travel to Mexico to visit Minita. To our delight, when she saw us she recognized us and smiled, but could only speak unintelligibly and hoarsely. They took good care of her, and although it was very sad to see her in that condition we comforted ourselves with the knowledge that our sister was not suffering, and was living a quiet and easy life. Now, I'm not saying she was happy, because her mind was not able to recognize the good things in life. Two years later we visited her again, but her condition had worsened, she was just eating and sleeping all day. God called Minita (may she rest in peace) in 2008 eighteen years after being diagnosed with Alzheimer's.

Carlos Magno Pompeyo

Carlos Magno Pompeyo was my youngest brother, and the only one who did not go to Callao High School. Instead, he studied at the Polytechnic of Peru in Lima. He graduated as an electrician and, again with the moral and financial support of Marina, managed to enroll at the Autonomous University of Mexico to pursue a career as a doctor of veterinary medicine. He graduated and received his degree with the specialization of cattle. He started working in his alma mater as a professor, and developed projects for many farmers in the region. He won the affection and respect of his students who later came to consult him about their problems in their farms. The youngest of the Egoavil's was also a very good athlete, he played handball with his students and, very occasionally, tennis. He met a young lady of the Mazatlán society and they married and had two daughters, Gabriela and Alicia. Gabriela obtained a BA in Business Administration and later her Master's degree. Gabriela married a Mexican gentleman named Lucio. Alicia, much like her father, graduated as a doctor in veterinary medicine. She had a small pets store with many Chihuahua dogs. Alicia promised her Aunt Elvia that when she was ready, she would send her a Chihuahua puppy. Until now Aunt Elvia is waiting for her puppy. Carlos and his family went to visit Chicago at the same time as I and my family did. It was a perfect family reunion; we all really enjoyed reminiscing about our time in Peru. Gringa cooked typical Peruvian dishes such as rice with chicken and cau-cau. My brother Carlos died in Chihuahua, Mexico from a rare disease that affected the brain. When I went to the funeral, I was filled with admiration of my brother to see his students there to say their goodbyes. They made farewell speeches that showed great affection and admiration for their former university professor. The day that I arrived in Chihuahua I went directly to the funeral home. I arrived at about eleven o'clock at night, and my niece Alicia greeted me first. She seemed surprised to see me, and said:

'I am so sorry Uncle Marco, for a moment I thought that you were my dad.' My brothers and I shared all of the same features, thick dark hair and darker eyes. I stayed for three days and two nights in Chihuahua. My niece Gabriela kindly offered me her room to sleep in. Before my departure, my niece Alicia took me to the university to see the laboratories where my brother used to teach. One laboratory had the name Professor Carlos Egoavil emblazoned on the front. Luciano, Gabriela's boyfriend, took me to the bus station to El Paso, Texas where I would fly back to West Palm Beach. A final funny story was told to me a few days after the funeral.

. I stayed 3 days and two nights in Chihuahua. My niece Gabriela gave me her room to sleep. Before leaving Chihuahua, Alicia took me to the University to show me the laboratories, where Carlos used to teach, one laboratory had the name of Professor Carlos Egoavil. Luciano, Gabriela's boyfriend took me to the bus station to El Paso, Texas where I would take my plane back to West Palm Beach.

One final story that somebody told me was that, a few days after the funeral, Gabriela was crying profusely, and wailed: 'Why did my dad have to die— why couldn't it have been my Uncle Marco instead, he was older!

When I reflect upon my life, I sincerely regret my estrangement from Efraim. I should have tried to communicate with him. I wish we had loved each other, as brothers should.

Lesson Thirteen: never fight with your brothers, love your brothers and always communicate with them to solve any problem between you and brother or sister.

CHAPTER NINE: MY MEDICAL HISTORY

My medical history began when I went to a doctor to ask for a heart certificate. This was to be used to apply to the Air Force of Peru, which I hoped would train me to become a pilot. But God had different ideas, my short stature and mother's eyes (she was very nearsighted and had advanced myopia) meant that I wasn't eligible to become a pilot. I bid farewell to my dream. I have been fortunate enough to enjoy relatively good health throughout my entire life. When I asked my grandchildren what genes they believe they inherited from me, among the answers were strength, steadfastness, intelligence, athleticism, ambition, a romantic notion, and religion. But the weakness was my sight. I have been shortsighted since high school. When the teacher wrote on the blackboard, I had to sit in the front row. That was not enough, and they soon took me to an optometrist who prescribed me lenses. At sixty years of age, I began having problems with my retina, and I went to a hospital in Boston that was considered the number one hospital in the nation. There, doctors operated on my retina. It had been wrinkled, and they tried to stretch it out. Unfortunately, the operation was not successful on my right eye— they could not stretch it out; they then tried the same to my left eye. A decade later, the doctor recommended an operation on the left eye because it was leaking. Thankfully, the surgery was successful and the leaking liquid was controlled, but I did not see (pun unintended) any marked improvement in my vision. When I was sixty years old, I was diagnosed with high cholesterol and started taking Lipitor. Soon, the diagnosis of high blood pressure also came, which I again controlled with pills. Currently, I take Crestor for cholesterol, and Lotrell and Carvedilol in low doses for blood pressure. One of the reasons for my fitness even in old age is that I played tennis every day for two hours with other senior citizens in the Riverwalk Community. I started playing tennis in 1989 when I started working at the NASA Langley Research Centre. We played

during lunchtime. In addition to playing tennis, I joined a group of employees of different nationalities who liked to play soccer (which all around the world is called football). Most players were in their forties, only four players were around my age. We played twice a week. When we lived in RiverWalk, a gated community in West Palm Beach which had eight clay tennis courts, I joined about fifteen players of my age to play tennis. I said to myself, now that I
am seventy-four years old I will try to play for four more years and then when I'm too old for tennis I'll play golf. It turned out that there was a skinny old man named Martin Skibee, a player of German descent, who was already seventy-eight years old. He was still enthusiastically playnig tennis and utterly unwilling to retire. Following his example, I changed my plans and said to myself: I will retire at the same age that Martin retires at. Martin was still playing at eighty-seven years old, the blessed man. Now, my friend Martin has not played for more than a month, and has hung his racket up on the wall. My plans changed when we moved from Riverwalk to the Two City Plaza Condominiums. Instead of playing tennis, I went to the gymn in my building. Martin's health failed him, and he passed away at ninety-two. I don't know if I will get to ninety-two, but I can say with an absolute certainty that, no matter how long, life is always too short. Can I live five more years to ninety-two, as Martin did? Perhaps, but only God knows when I will be cremated and
my ashes kept in a box in a local Cemetery of West Palm Beach. Those are my wishes that I have told my wife to follow when I pass away. To summarise, my vision is very bad in my right eye (which I therefore consider my bad eye) so I read the newspaper and type on my computer using, primarily, my left eye. I think that my height influenced my shyness, but my shyness did not have much effect on my life. Strengthened through my life of sports, my character allowed me to get whatever I wanted. I had many girlfriends, like Tom Sawyer I enjoyed my first kiss at seven years old. I mention this as a lesson for future dads— it

could happen that your little boy is, without your knowledge, is kissing someone on the sly. Boys and little girls know that sex exists at an early age and this is true since the beginning of time. My wifey Elvia says: "Today a youth at twelve years old knows more about sex than I knew when I was 20 years old." Tennis helped me keep my health, but had little effect on my blood pressure. I do not know why, but my pulse is kind of low, in the range of the fifties. My brother in law Eddy told me:
'You have a low pulse because of the ball.' I asked:
'What ball?' Eddy responded:
'The ball of years that you have.' I do not know what he was talking about.
My doctors tell me not to worry, a pulse of fifty is acceptable. If I do not exercise, my pulse goes down. But the days that I go to the gym my pulse goes up from fifty up to sixty. Two days ago my pressure was 124-75-66. Yesterday and today I did not exercise, when I measured my blood pressure and resulted to be 139-72-52. To conclude, these figures confirm that if I run the tread mill for thirty minutes daily my pressure and pulse improve. The lesson for my grandchildren to enjoy good health is:

Lesson Fourteen: pray before bedtime and you will sleep well. Practice sports, eat wisely, never drink liquor in excess, in your senior years of age take a small glass of red wine every night, and practice tennis or golf every single day.

CHAPTER TEN: MUSIC AND BOLEROS

Everyone loves music, and I am certainly no exception. After listening to a song that I like I feel extremely grateful to God, and that I want to do something good in this world. Many times, my eyes have filled not with tears of sadness, but of joy. I sometimes wish that I could sing professionally, but God did not gift me with particularly good ears. In any case, I am happy that God gave musical talent to all of my favorite opera singers, such as Pavarotti and Placido Domingo. My favorite American singers include Frank Sinatra, Doris Day, Nat King Cole, Perry Como, Andy Russell, Ella Fitzgerald, and Peggy Lee. I am also partial to singers of Boleros such as Los Panchos, Pedro Vargas, Leo Marini, and Lucho Gatica. I love both classical and popular music of each region of the world. I find Paraguayan music very beautiful. Though I do enjoy listening to classical music and operas, I devote most of my time listening to American 'pop' music. My childhood radio delivered the first American tunes to my ears, which were also exposed to Peruvian waltzes sung by the likes of Jesus Vasquez, the Morochucos, and Los Embajadores Criollos. They did not attract me much; I found them melancholic and sad. I began listening to North American music when I was in high school. The music was transmitted by radio in the music box by the Bolivian Jorge Pelaez Rioja. It was on at 1 and 10 pm my time, and everyone in the house knew to leave me alone then. From listening to songs from films, I grew to love Doris Day and Frank Sinatra. I watched the film 'Tea for Two' five times in six months, such was my love for it. I also watched 'Leven Anchors' four times. My favorite song writers were (and still are) Cole Porter, Irving Berlin, Jerome Kerr, Rogers and Hammerstein, amongst many others. Another reason that I love music is that my favorite singer from the 1950s to present day is Andy Russell. He was a North Aerican singer of Mexican parents, and he would sing his songs in both English and Spanish. Much to my dismay, not many people know who Andy Russell was, so I would like to tell you, reader, a bit about his life. Russel rose to fame at around the same time as Frank Sinatra and Perry Como. In 1947, he replaced Frank Sinatra on the radio program 'Your Hit Parade'. Andy Russell sold gold records (i.e more than one million copies) of the subsequent songs: Besame Mucho, What a Difference a Day means which is the English version of a Bolero created by Maria Grever, Cuando Vuelva a Tu Lado, Magic is the Moonlight, Muñequita Linda, and Amor, Amor, Amor. Russel was hired by Radio El Sol and worked in Lima, for three days in a row. I would listen to him singing my favorite songs every single night. He was presented with a young Mexican comedian named Chicho Gordillo. Chico would humorously mimick Andy, and they would end the programme singing: You Belong to My Heart, as a duet. Andy workedi n Mexico and Argentino in accordance with his many contracts during the 1950s and 1960s. Andy Russell (may he rest in peace) died at age seventy two in Los Angeles. All of my grandchildren certainly have their own favorite songs, the only legacy that I can leave them are the lyrics in English and Spanish of songs. I often sing it with them as a duet; my granddaughter Ariana follows my singing of 'Tu me Acostrumbraste' very easily. When they hear the songs that I played them, they will think fondly that their Abuelo Marco loves that song. These songs are also for grandparents such as me who would listen to boleros in their youth, it can fill them with a desire to help everyone again. Occasionally, I hear some of my favorite songs on YouTube, and all of the emotions from my youth mentioned above come flooding back to me. If I were to make a list of my favorite songs, there would be eleven on that list:

1. 'Star Dust', Hoagy Carmichael
2. 'As Time Goes By', from Casablanca
3. 'What a Difference a Day Means', Maria Grever
4. 'Amor, Amor, Amor', Gabriel Ruiz

5. 'You Belong to My Heart' ('Solamente Una Vez'),
    Agustin Lara
6. 'The Very Thought of You', Ray Noble
7. 'Muñequita Linda' ('Magic is the Moonlight'), Maria
    Grever
8. 'Moonlight Serenade' ('Serenata a la Luz de la Luna'),
    Glenn Miller
9. 'Sabor a Mi' ('Be True to Me'), Alvaro Carrillo
10. 'Tea for Two', Youmans Vincent.
11. Adios Muchachos' ('I get Ideas'), Argentine Tango.
     Due to copyright restrictions, I dare not to publish the
     lyrics of those

songs, instead I have decided to give some details about
the authors who created them. The information was taken
from the Free Encyclopedia Wikipedia, and some additional
details taken from YouTube.

1. 'STARDUST'

'Star Dust' was composed by Hoagy Carmichael in 1927,
with lyrics added in 1929 by Mitchell Parish. Hoagy
Carmichael was born on the 22 of November, 1899, and
died on the 27 of December, 1981. He was an American
composer, pianist, singer, actor, and bandleader.
Numbered amongst his well known songs are 'Star Dust',
'Georgia on My Mind', 'The Nearness of You', and 'Heart
and Soul'. Those are four of the most listened-to American
songs of all time. One of the first singers who popularised
the songs was the young baritone Bing Crosby, who
recorded them in 1931. The following year, many
orchestras had recorded 'Star Dust'. Popular versions were
also recorded by Louis Armstrong, Tommy Dorsey, and Tex
Beneke Orchestra with Glenn Miller. Frank Sinatra, Doris
Day, and Nat King Cole became very famous in Latin
America. In the sixties, I heard a a song in Spanish by Andy
Russell, but I cannot now locate that particular song,
unfortunately.

2. 'AS TIME GOES BY'

This song was from the film Casablanca, which was written by Herman Hupheld in 1931. It became famous when the pianist Sam (Dooley Wilson) sang it in the film. The version that I like best was sung by Rod Stewart and Christy Heinim, you can find it on the internet if you search: 'As Time Goes By', Rod Stewart and Christy Heinim. Other singers who I like and sang this song are: Vic Damone, Doris Day, and Frank Sinatra.

3. 'CUANDO VUELVA A TU LADO'

The music and lyrics to this song are by Maria Grever. She was born in Guanajuato, Mexico, on the 16th of August 1894, and she died on the 15th of December 1951. She was the first Mexican who became a famous composer. At six, her family moved to her father's hometown Sevilla, and she studied music in France with Claude Debussy and Franz Lenhard. At twelve, she returned to Mexico and continued her musical studies at the College of Music. When she was twenty-two, she married an American 'gringo' manager of an oil company They moved to New York City, where she lived for the rest of her life. Grever wrote over eight-hundred songs, most of which were boleros. They became famous worldwide. The first song which became internationally famous was the boler 'Jurame' which was sung by the tenor Jose Mojica. She then wrote the bolers 'Volvere', 'Te Quiero Dijiste', and 'Muñequita Linda' which is known in America as 'Magic is the Moonlight'. 'Cuando Vuelva a Tu Lado' became internationally notorious when the English version was recored as: 'What a Difference a Day Made'. There are excellent versions of this song in both English and Spanish; the ones that I love best were recorded by Andy Russel and Dinah Washington. Grever won a Grammy Award for the song, which was inducted into the Grammy Hall of Fame. Maria Grever died in 1951 in New York, and her remains were transported to Mexico City at her request.

4. 'AMOR, AMOR, AMOR'

The music to this song was written by Gabriel Ruiz and the lyrics by Ricardo Lopez Mende. The lyrics in English were written by Sunny Skylar. The Mexican composer was born in Guadalagar on the 9th of March 1908, and he died on the 31st of January 1999. The North American version was recorded by Bing Crosby and Andy Russell. Julio Iglesias also recorded th song, and gave it a lighter pace.

5. 'SOLAMENTE UNA VEZ'

Both the music and lyrics of this song were written by Augustin Lara. Lara was born in Tlacotalpan, Veracruz, in 1900. He died in 1970. During his life, he had two wives: Maria Felix and Rocio Duran. When he was young, the Lara family moved to Coyoacan County in Mexico City. When his mother died, Augustin and his brothers went to live in a nursing home that their aunt owned. It was there that Augustin first becan to study music. His first composition was 'Marucha', which was written in honour of one of his first great loves. In 1927, he worked in a cabaret club. 1928 saw him go to work for the tenor Juan Arvizu as a composer and accompanist. Lara began a successful career in radio in 1930. In addition to those careers, he worked as an actor and composer for many films. In Cuba, Lara's first work was a complete and utter failure due to the strenuous political situation there. Later, he went to work in South America, and he became very successful through songs such as 'Solamente Una Vez', which was composed in Buenos Aires. His songs Veracruz, Tropicana, and Pecadora only heightened his fame. In the beginning of 1940, Lara was very well known in Spain. In 1965, the Spanish dictator General Francisco Franco gave him a house in Granada, to show Spain's appreciation for his music which focused on Spanish cities and issues. The songs were: 'Toled', 'Cuerdas de mi Guitarra', 'Granada', 'Sevilla', and 'Madrid'. Lara received many other honours and awards from other countries all around the globe. In 1968, Lara's health deteriorated rapidly, and an accident which fractured his pelvis aggravated his frail condition. On the 6th of November, 1970, Augustin Lara died. His remains were buried in Mexico City. He wrote over 700 songs throughout his life.

6. 'THE VERY THOUGHT OF YOU'

'The Very Thought of You' was published in 1942, music and lyrics written by Ray Noble. In addition to the success of his own orchestra and the singer Al Bowlly playing his song, Bing Crosby recorded his own version. A decade later, the song was still being played on the radio. In 1946, Andy Russel recorded a version, and Doris Day sang it in the 1950 film 'Man with a Horn'. Kirk Douglas played the jazz trumpeter Bix Beiderbecke. An instrumental version of the song is played in the film 'Casablanca', in the scene where Sascha kisses Rick Blaine on the cheek. Singers of jazz and pop such as Ella Fitzgerald, Frank Sinatra, Nat King Cole, carmen McRae, and Billy Holiday recorded their own versions, too.

7. 'MUNEQUITA LINDA'

Maria Grever wrote this touching song. It was not, as the lyrics imply, written for a lover, but was in fact for a small girl who had passed away. Maria was thinking of her, and said 'sometimes I hear a dicine echo wrapped in the breeze', and from this she composed the song. The girl's mother says that the song brings her comfort, and when she listens to it she can imagine that her daughter is still with her.

8. 'MOONLIGHT SERENADE'

The Spanish version of this song is entitled: 'Serenata a la Luz de la Luna'. The music is by Glenn Miller and the lyrics by Mitchell Parrish. An instrumental arrangement of this song was an instant success, and became the theme tune of the Glenn Miller Orchestra. what stands out most in this song is the lone clarinet that is followed by a saxophone section. This is considered classic Glenn Miller. This song was one of the first examples of the fragrance, the essence, the style, per say, that the big bands would have in the mid-twentieth century. Frank Sinatra's version is lovely, as is Andy Russel's Spanish version.

9. 'SABOR A MI'

Alvaro Carrillo composed this song. He was a Mexican man born in San Juan, Cacahuatepec Oaxaca, on the 2nd of December, 1921. He died in a car accident on the 3rd of April 1969. During his lifetime, he wrote over three-hundred songs. In 1945, he graduated from agronomist, but soon left engineering to compose music. The famous Japanese singer Yoshiro Hiriishi recorded the song, and his version became an international success. Other notorious singers have also recorded this song, such as Javier Solis, Jose and Doris Day (who recorded this song in English, entitled: 'Be True To Me'.

10. 'TEA FOR TWO'

Vincent Youmans wrote the music to this song and Irving Caesar wrote the lyrics. 'Tea for Two' is a song from the Broadway musical 'No, No Annette'. In the 50s, the film 'Tea for Two', with Doris Day and Gordon MacRae starring as the protagonists, came to theatres. When I first saw this film in Lima, I liked it so much that I watched it a total of five times in six months. My platonic love that I described in the chapter of Shyness and Aggressiveness was very much like Doris Day. At least, they had the same haircut, so whenever I see Doris Day I remember the breathtaking, beautiful girl in red. The same often happens when I listen to the song 'Tea for Two.' 'Tea For Two" became very popular, and was recorded by the most famous orchestras and instrumentalists of the time. It was one of the songs that was played on the Lawrence Welk Show more than 1000 times in different episodes, transmitted on television. In the United States, some sixty-seven other television shows played 'Tea for Two'; its immense popularity stands as a testament to its greatness.

11. 'ADIOS MUCHACHOS'

The music to this song was written by Julio Cesar Sanders
and the lyrics by Cesar Felipe Verdini. It was originally an
Argentine tango created in 1927. Carlos Gardel sang the
song, Andy Russell sang it in Spanish, and Tony Martin
sang it in English under the title "I get ideas." In 1954, when
I was in my last year of Mechanical Engineering at the
National University of Engineering and with some fellow
peers celebrating an important occasion, I ended up at a
local bar in Lima. We drank about a dozen beers, and
someone started singing Peruvian waltzes. Suddenly,
someone asked:

'Do you know: 'Adios Muchachos'?' Raul Montalvo, Manuel
Carranza, and I said of course we do! I knew the whole
song by heart, and because the others only knew bits and
pieces of it, there were times when I only I was singing. I
sang it in the style of Andy Russell, singing 'Goodbye Boys,
Companions of my Life' with all of my lungs. When the song
finished, Raul said:

'Marco was so excited and emotional tonight.' I had to
agree.

**Lesson Fifteen: Sing to, dance to, learn, and most
importantly enjoy music.**

CHAPTER ELEVEN: TWO BRIEF LESSONS

These two brief lessons were not directly a part of my life. Rather, they come from a book that I read as though it were the Bible, or perhaps a book of modern history. The first is in regards to parent-children relationships and behavior. Never, under any circumstances, should a child disrespect their parents. They should never say 'Mom, I hate you'. It saddens God every time a child does so, and I hope that the child will soon realize that and correct their behavior. Metaphorically, the devil dominates the child when they proclaim their detestation of their parents. If you ever say that, I ask of you to remember the fifth commandment, 'honor thy mother and thy father'. Then, you must beg for forgiveness of your parents and of God. I do not know whether the Catholic Church influenced this belief, or if I read it in a book, or even saw it in a movie. But I know that it is a fundamental truth of life. Always be good to your parents, for they gave you life and only ever want the best for you.

Lesson Sixteen: you shall love and respect your parents above all things.

The next lesson for my grandchildren is a piece of advice for how to raise their children. That is, it is more of a lesson for parents. I know many families in which the parents give absolutely everything to their child, regardless of whether or not they can afford it. Often, the result is a selfish, self-oriented child who believes that the world revolves around him or her. As a parent, you must, obviously, give your child what they need and all of the love in your heart, for you can never have too much love. But I urge you to be wary when giving your children material things, make sure it is not an excess. Instead, take your child to a museum or to the park, spend time with them. Those are the things that count. Love and time.

Lesson Seventeen: do not spoil your child with material things; enrich them with spiritual gifts instead.

CHAPTER TWELVE: FAMILY REUNIONS

My memories of our family reunions are perfectly preserved in the many photos that are always taken. I am proud to number such intelligent, successful, and most importantly happy men and women in my family. Our good health is best illustrated in the oldest of us all at eighty-nine, the writer of this book. Here is a brief synopsis of my family tree:

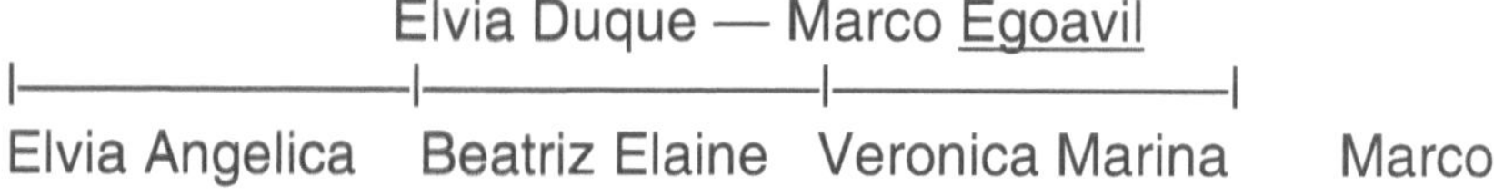

Elvia Duque — Marco Egoavil

|————————|————————|————————|

Elvia Angelica   Beatriz Elaine   Veronica Marina   Marco

Elvia Egoavil — Dan Strutzel

|————————|————————|

Kyra Angelica   Jeremy Daniel   Camden Anthony

Beatriz Egoavil — Doug Gerdts

|————————|————————|————————|

Gabriela Elaine   Veronica Ann   Grant   Lola

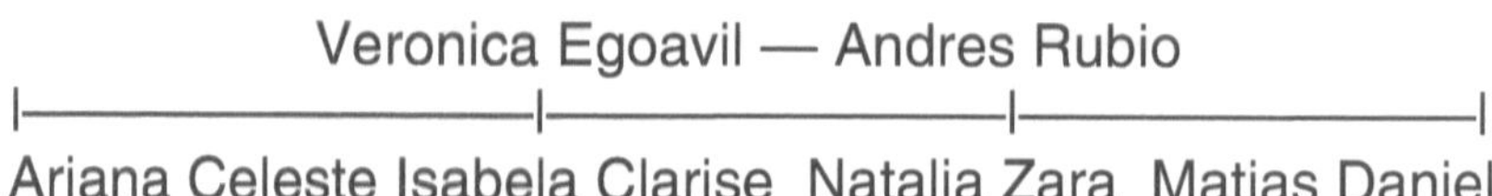

Veronica Egoavil — Andres Rubio

|————————|————————|————————|

Ariana Celeste Isabela Clarise Natalia Zara Matias Daniel

Marco Egoavil Jr — Brian Perrin

My son has no children, but he and his husband have two dogs (Rocco and Bruno) whom they treat like their own flesh and blood.

Gabriela Gerdts — Justin Detweiler
|————————————|
Brielle Marie   Olivia Leigh

Our very first family reunion was in Orlando, Florida. Veronica rented a couple of houses to accommodate the whole family. After eating a hearty breakfast, we went to Disneyland. All of the families enjoyed themselves immensely. The villas had a pool, which we used every day. It was then that we began the annual tradition of taking a family photo. When Veronica and Andres bought a house in Candlewood Isle, New Fairfield, Connecticut, it became the location for our family reunions. For my eightieth birthday, Veronica organized a fabulous celebration. She hosted the first 'Egoavilympics' which was a competition between two teams. It consisted of playing basketball, sack races, a water balloon toss, swimming, and tug-of-war. Then, there was a concert. The grandchildren sang the soundtrack to 'The Sound of Music' while their Abuela Elvia dressed up with a hat and guitar as Julie Andrews. There was then a parody of the action film 'Batman', with Dan as Batman, myself as Robin, and Beatriz as the Joker. After, everyone applauded wildly. A gala dinner was served on the porch overlooking the lake. Speeches and toasts were made, celebrating myself and my life. At the end of dinner, I delivered a speech that I had prepared (using the methods taught to me at the Toastmasters club of course):

1. **Thank you all.** I never thought, even in my wildest dreams, that we would all be here today, celebrating my eightieth birthday. I'd like to thank my children and their families for being here, and my beautiful wife. Chispitas, I'm very glad you're with us and please tell Gringa, Eddy, and Cesar that I wish they could have been here too. Thank you.

2. When I was a young man, **I did not know what I was doing.** All of this before us is possible because God placed a girl, who also did not know what she was doing, into my life when we married forty-six years ago.

3. **I'd like to give credit where credit is due.** I wish to thank God for helping me to have all of this wonderful family. My wife and I mustn't take all the glory; let us thank Don Quintin and Doña Josefina, Fred and Lynn, and all of the other grandparents who have helped to make this family. I'd also like to give a special thanks to Veronica and Andres for planning this perfect day.

4. **Life is short.** This may seem ironic, coming from me who turns eighty today. My youngest grandchild Matias is three years old, so he has to live seventy-seven more years until he is in my position. That may seem like a long time, especially to my young grandchildren, but believe me when I say that life is short. To Gabby, who will go to college for four years and have the time of her life, life is short. The years will fly by. For Andres, who works, life is also short. Life is short for all of us, regardless of age.

5. In life, **it is important to have goals.** All of the men and women here have planned their life with necessary goals to achieve what they want. I did the same when I finished high school, and, at the time, my goals were simple: a) get a degree in engineering

in the United States. b) get married and have eleven children to make a football team (here, everyone laughed).

6. Getting a **degree** in the United States was not an easy process: I applied three times to get a scholarship, first when I finished high school, second after I got my degree in Mechanical Engineering in Lima, and third after gaining industrial experience whilst working as a mechanical engineer for six years. Finally, after fourteen yours, I got a scholarship to study in the United States. I was awarded the Fulbright scholarship to study at the University of Notre Dame. I said to myself that when I got a

master's degree at Notre Dame, then I could marry.

7. I am forever grateful to **God.** When I told my friend Sam Corcarán in Boca Raton how I married Elvia Duque, a story that you all know well, he told me: 'Marco, it was your destiny. God put Elvia in your life.' To my Elvita and Veronica I say the same: 'God put Dan and Andres, respectively, in your life. Beatrice: I believe that God has something special for you. Believe me, life is short, but God will give you what you want and your dreams will come true. Have faith in God.

8. **Gaby's Career:** I have been talking to Gaby about which career she should study. A few months ago, she told me that she would like to study Business Administration. She wants to be like her Aunt Veronica and Uncles Marco and Andres. She told me, 'Grandpa, I want to be a millionaire.' I told her that she could be absolutely anything she dreamed of. Veronica, Kyra, Ariana, Isabela, and Natalia: you can be and do whatever you want in life.

9. Finally, let me tell all of you that, today, I feel like a
    millionaire. Now, my bank account may disagree. But
    my children and my eleven grandchildren, I have a
    special relationship with each and every one, all make
    me feel like a millionaire because I love you. I am a
    millionaire rich in body and soul because God takes
    care of me and has granted me good health and love.
    Thank you God for giving me this wonderful family.

That was the end of my speech. So, you ask, what is the
lesson for my grandchildren in regards to these family
gatherings? Well, I hope that they themselves organize an
annual reunion when their parents are eighty years old, and
that they will play games and have fun like we did.

**Lesson Eighteen: Try and organize an annual family
reunion.**

CHAPTER THIRTEEN: HOLIDAYS AND TRIPS

As a professor at the University of Puerto Rico, the summer holidays were very interesting. This was because I was eligible to apply to a program of the American Society of Education to work in one of the most famous American Engineering Laboratories. So, I worked in the National Livermore Laboratory in California, at the NASA Lewis Research Centre in Cleveland, Ohio, and the Arnold U.S Air Force Station in Tennessee, all for ten weeks at a time. Chronologically, the most important trips in my life were:

New York City
At eighteen years old, as a sailor crewman from the Peruvian Steamship Corporation, I travelled to New York City to fetch a Liberty ship that the Peruvian Government had bought from the United States. Here is an excerpt of a letter detailing the trip which I wrote to my granddaughter Veronica:

On the 25th of January, 1949, the entire crew of the sip Napo travelled from Lima to New York by plane. We stayed at the Cornish Arms Hotel on 23rd Street, 8th Avenue. There were issues with the contract between Peru and the United States, so we stayed at the hotel for two and a half months, enjoying an impromptu vacation the the Big Apple. Most of us had never been before. I was the only sailor who could speak English. We went out every afternoon to the Rockefeller Centre ice- skating rink to look at the gringuitas (blonde girls) who were there. I would order food for everyone from restaurants; we usually went to an automatic restaurant on 42nd Street because you saw the food through a window, slotted in coins, and the window opened revealing a sandwich, or delicious apple pie. We visited all of the museums in the city. We didn't, however, see any Broadway shows, because it was far too expensive.

South America

This was my sailing adventure at sea. We left New York for Philadelphia where we received a few loads that consisted of large boxes, whose insides were a mystery to us. Someone told us that they were machinery. During the first two days of the trip, I was so seasick that I threw up twice an hour in my cabin. I couldn't eat for the two days, and when I finally served myself some soup on the third day, the Argentinian meat floating around in oil revolted me. It was there that I picked up the habit of blowing the fat away and pouring out most of the oil. The seasickness would suddenly appear whenever we left a port, but would eventually dissipate. After a week in Philadelphia, we went on to Galveston, Texas, where we picked up yet more mysterious cargo. Our next stop was Nuevita, Cuba. I met and made friends with several young Cubans who told me that they wanted to be musicians. Almost all of them played an instrument; everyone belonged to a band which gave public performances. They were always very happy, wih smiles on their faces, every time I saw them. All of this was before Castro. From what I've been told, now young Cubans that aspire to be musicians are only half of what they were before Castro. The dictator Fidel Castro remains unaware that he has destroyed the character and cheerful spirit of the Cubans. The ship received a load of minerals destined for Santos, Brazil. After a twenty-five-day trip throughout the Caribbean Sea and the Atlantic Ocean, we arrived at Santos. We stayed there for fifteen days, unloading and loading bananas that we would take to Buenos Aires, Argentina. Us sailors were working, for eight hours a day from Monday to Friday, painting the walls of a room with diesel engines. When we were anchored in the harbor, we had the freedom to head ashore and explore the city, after work of course. The Brazilians had the same joyous and vivacious spirit of the Cubans. Santos was ten times larger than Nuevitas, and soon we were approached by some boys who offered us cigarettes. i was an eighteen year old boy, I was still very innocent and simple-minded, so I said:

'I do not smoke, thank you.' I noticed that none of my colleagues bought cigarettes. Later, they explained to me that the boys were selling marijuana cigarettes. I like to think that my guardian angel had led me to the right decision. When we arrived in Buenos Aires, we went to see a movie at the 'Teatro Colon'. A guide lit the way to our seats with a lantern. My friend Juan Ulloa whispered to me that the guide wanted a tip. Juan took half an Argentine peso out of his pocket and gave it to the guide. The guide looked at the coin, and exclaimed angrily that we were 'very cheap'. Juan turned red as a tomato. The ship crossed the Strait of Magellan at the South Pole during the trip. We anchored in front of Valparaiso, Chile, only to leave right away across the strait. A week later we arrived in Callao. Everyone was asking eachother if they were going to continue travelling on the ship, we had been told that the next trip was to Europe. Although the trip had been very interesting, and we had visited new cities and new cultures, I felt a thrill to say:

'No. i am staying in Callao because I plan to go to college to study mechanical engineering.'

North of Peru

At the National Engineering University a travel vacation was available to the North of Peru. It was a very well-organized trip, for a few days we visited the cities of Piria and Trujillo.

At the Museum of Trujillo, there was a section describing the sexual life of the Incas in Peru. This sexual aspect surprised me, but it is a part of life. For example, in Madrid there is a vast amount of Picasso paintings featuring the female nude. This isn't wrong, you should jsut be careful wehn taking children to such places.

Centre of Peru

During vacation at the National Engineering University a student trip to Central Peru was organized to explore the city of Huancayo. We arrived by train to Oroya, which was more that 1000 meters above sea level. Walking at the streets of the city, I bought a few tasty pancakes from a street vendor which I ate eagerly. Half an hour later I felt very ill, and soon I was vomiting. Diarrhea overpowered me, and I was miserable both nights. I remember being very grateful to my friend Manuel Garranza, who helped me and took me to the American Hospital of La Oroya at midnight. They sent me to sleep with some pills. When I woke up the next day, I had a terrible headache and was still vomiting, so it was decided that I would return to Lima. My friend Sergio Barba offered to accompany. Sergio dropped me off at my house and he returned to Oroya. A week later I felt much better, but noticed that there was a strange humming nose in my left ear. I went to the doctor, who diagnosed an injury to the inner ear. This caused me to not be able to detect exactly the decibels of the human voice in that ear. If someone were to whisper something to me, I would have to ask them to do so in my right (good) ear. So, whenever I went to the movies I sat to the left of whoever accompanied me. I still do that when I go to the movies now, my wife sits to the right of me. The ear injury is, unfortunately, permanent, despite my many appointments with ear specialists. They daid that the inner ear is too complicated and that they could do nothing to cure it.

Machu Pichu and Cuzco

Approximately twenty engineering students arrived at Cuzco by plane and stayed in a hotel. We were at an

altitude of 3,000 meters above sea level, and I can recall not being able to run because I would get out of breath almost immediately. Remembering the sickness I had experienced in Oroya, I was cautious with my food. The next day we went to visit the famous Machu Pichu. The city of the Incas is so famous that I'm sure many of you will visit Machu Pichu at some time in your life. The fame of this city is based on the construction of the walls of houses, temples, and Inca fortresses. They used irregular shaped stones which were cut to fit together perfectly. A needle could not fit between two stones. All of the walls are very stable and unaffected by earthquakes. At the time, cement did not exist, so their strength is remarkable. One of the less plausible theories as to how the walls were built is that super intelligent extraterrestrials constructed the city. Somehow, I do not think that that is the case. At the National Engineering University our vibrations professor was Engineer René Guevara. He was from Cuzco and had a ranch outside of the city, which he invited us to spend a day at. It was a perfect day, with sunshine and fresh air. Lunch was served in the garden, and consisted of all kinds of meats: red meat, steak, pork, chicken, and goat. There was also beer for anyone who was thirsty. After we had finished lunch, the engineer's wife called for our attention. 'I have seen that some of you like the beer, but you are drinking it wrong. I insist that you all take at least one more beer and drink it correctly.' She gave us not one, not two, but three more rounds of beer despite our protests. After that, we were all very happy and sleepy. The younger brother of Professor Guevara was a famous violinist, known internationally, and he said:
'To control this sudden emotion, we shall play a game of football.' We formed two teams, and started playing, forgetting about the altitude for the moment. Energized by the beer, we played one of the best games of my life.

An Important Conference

A Peruvian student, who had studied engineering in the United States, gave a lecture at General Assembly in Callao High School. The conference impressed me, so when he finished I decided to emulate the speaker's steps and girst began to consider a career in the United States. The first step that I took was to go to the North American Peruvian Cultural Institute in Lima, and I requested a scholarship to study mechanical engineering. The rest of this story is described in the letter to my granddaughter Veronica in the chapter: 'Shyness and Agressiveness'. But I digress. That conference marked the moment I decided to go after my dream.

Return Journey to Lima

My return trip to Lima, having achieved my Masters degree in Mechanical Engineering obtained at the University of Notre Dame, consisted of visits to Mexico, Acapulco, Managua (the capital of Nicaragua), Panama, and Cali, Colombia. That was where I met my wife, and our story is described in the chapter: 'How I Married a Colombian Girl'.

Wolverhampton, England

During the academic year of 1967-1968 while I was working at the National Engineering University, I won an UNESCO scholarship to study in Wolverhampton Technical Teachers College and the University of Illinois Urbana Champaign. I took courses that taugt me how to teach courses of Mechanical Engineering in the field of Thermal Sciences. I applied everything that I learned there when I later taught Thermodynamics, a course which I have taught at least one-hundred times. When Elvia and I married several of her sisters did not attend the marriage, so we visited Cali to see them. For the first time, I met her sisters Rubelia, Amparo, Rita, and Alonzo. Unfortunately, I was not able to meet her brothers Father Aristobulo (may he rest in peace) who died after a battle with cancer last year, and Cesar who lived in Bogota. We travelled with our two daughters Elvita and Beatriz. The UNESCO scholarship enabled me to follow a programme of theoretical studies in pedagogy, and other practical visits to internationally known factories, such as Rolls Royce. There, they showed us how engineers design gas turbines in Rugby, England. At the end of the course, we went to Paris for a week. We were accompanied by Dr Peter Ovadia, an UNESCO expert with whom I worked in Lima. One night, after visiting all of the tourist locations in Paris, we left the girls asleep in the hotel and went to see the Lido show. We told a hotel concierge that the girls were alone. She assured us that she would look after them if they woke up The second part of the UNESCO scholarship was at the University of Illinois, where we followed a similar programme as in England. When we were in Urbana-Champaign, we recieved the sad news of the deaths of my dad Antonio and Elvia's dad, Don Jesus. Both men died only days apart. I think that these first trips that Elvia and I took as a marriaed couple strengthened our relationship. For example, Elvia initially wanted a small family, while I wanted a large one. When we returned to Lima, Elvia suggested having a third child, perhaps a boy Instead, Veronica Marina was born on the first of November. She was born with so much hair that it was obvious she took after me and the Egoavil side of the family. When Elvita was born she had a bald head like a billiard ball. Beatriz was also born virtually hairless, but her hair was black and she looked like me. The following year the little boy that God had been saving for us was born, Marco Antonio Jr..

Lima

I lived in Hampton in 1988. I went on an eight day trip to Lima, having not been there for 26 years. My wife and children did not go with me as it was too expensive. I stayed with my cousin Leonor. I presented two lectures on my specialty design of wind tunnels at the Society of Engineers of Peru and at the National Engineering University. It was an utter pleaser to dine with my colleagues, the ME54s of the UNI. The saddest part of the trip was when I learnt that some of y friends had died, including my best friend Sergia Barba. I visited his widow, Judith, who explained that Sergio died a three months after having cancer of the mouth. I visited my friend Macario Rojas, who had an illness of the prostate and bladder. Macario (may he rest in peace) died the following year, another victim of cancer.

Germany
In 2001, NASA approved my trip to Heidelberg, Germany, to deliver a lecture on the design of a fuel injector with a stable flame. I asked permission of NASA to take a vacation and extend my trip ten more days. We signed up for a Globus Tour of a ten day visit in European countries. We joined the tour in Frankfurt, Germany, then Switzerland, Austria, in Italy we visited Florence, Venice, and Rome. We spent a day in Monte Carlo and finally two days in Paris exploring the wonders of the city. We returned to Frankfurt on the midnight train. The plane from Frankfurt to Norfolk took us towards our house in Hampton, VA.

Norweigan Cruise by the Caribbean
In March of 2012, to celebrate our 50th anniversary, my wife Elvia and I took a cruise. It was a wonderful trip, which I described in the following email to my children:

Dearest Elvita, Beatriz, Veronica, and Marco,
After seven days of cruising the Caribbean, I feel as though I am qualified to heartily recommend it. As soon as you have time, you should all go on a cruise. I have found that it does a world of good to the body and mind. However, I don't know how well you would fare Veronica, given your motion sickness (ironic, considering that your middle name is Marina!). The passengers on the cruise with us were of all ages, babies to little ninety year old ladies in wheelchairs. There were two pools, a volleyball and basketball court, and a movie theatre (which we unfortunaly could not try out due to a lack of time). It was seven blissful days of eating tasty food, having fun, watching musicals,

meeting friendly people, and -the best bit -uninterrupted sleep! On the first day, we went to a restaurant. The ship The Norwegian Sun had the grand total of eleven restaurants, four with specialised menus which cost extra. We signed up to go to one that had an orchestra, but it turned out to be a trio playing music softly in the background. Throughout the trip, we went to three of the restaurants. All of the food was excellent, and the service efficient. One day, they arranged a table with twenty different chocolate cakes for desert- and you served yourself. Your mom's sweet tooth was put to good use that day. On the last day, in the Bahamas, we had lunch on the beach. It was a very well organised picnic. Every day at seven-thirty, there were Broadway-style shows with fabulous dancers and professional singers. They were famous artists who had worked on Broadway shows such as Shouts, Cats, and Evita. Twice, famous comedians from Las Vegas entertained us with jokes that made the audience fall of their seats fom laughter. Near the pool area, they set up a dance floor and bands played rock and roll an, much to our delight, Latin music. Many young couples took to the floor. At night, there were three pianists who took turns playing, in shifts of usually an hour, but sometimes two. There was a very good pianist-singer named Joe, whom I liked a lot because he played music of the 50s. We went to the cities Conzumel-Mexico, Cayman Islands, Ocho Rios-Jamaica, Great Stirrup, and Gay- Bahamas. We sailed for two days and two nights. The first shops in the port were three jewellers. In Cozumel we went to the city and had lunch. We had hamburgers with fries and cokes, which cost 25$! (In McDonalds, it's only 6$). In Jamaica, two colourfully dressed women, one with a cushion on her chest and the other with a pillow on her lower back, moved gracefully with great skill and to the pace of Jamaican music played by three musicians. As you know, your mom makes friends very easily. One of the first friends that she made was a Peruvian lady named Jacqueline Chang, who sold products in the duty free shop of the ship. We met eight Peruvian employees and three Colombians, and we chatted with other retired couples, some of whom we found out took cruises twice a year. They had seen half of the world. One night, your mother was tired and told me to collect some photographs at about ten pm. I picked up the photos, and on my way back to our cabin I passed many halls and a room which caught my eye, because the sound of laughter echoed out of it. I entered, and there was a small theatre where people were playing games instructed by a few directors. They asked the audience to perform several tasks. One was to have men walk around him- in heels. So, the women gave the men their heels and they cheerfully donned them and strutted around. The directors then chose the winner. He then asked if anyone had a tattoo of a vertical lie on their back. A beautiful blonde girl next to me asked if I did. Chuckling, I answered no. My time came when the director asked if anyone wore dentures, and the girl grabbed me by the hand and led me to to the stage. I took off my false teeth and showed them to the director. The blonde girl high-fived me. Then, they called for a:

'Man and a woman to exchange shirt and blouse,'. Another beautiful girl took my hand and led me to the stage, and we exchanged shirts. I couldn't stop laughing as I got off of the stage. Then, they asked for a couple to show them the most romantic position they had ever done. The blonde girl and her boyfriend ran to the stage and showed everyone a passionate embrace, which I shan't describe here because this is, after all, a book for my grandchildren. Let your imagination run amuck. After that, they wanted a woman with her bra. The blonde girl wriggled hers off and ran to the stage with the bra grasped in her hand like a victory flag. I do not know who won, because I realised that I had been gone from my cabin for half an hour,so I left. I ran through the empty halls of the ship (for it was now about eleven pm) laughing like a madman. When I arrived back at the cabin, I told your mom that it was the most hilarious experience I had ever had, and that I had enjoyed it very much. There

was a tax free shop on the ship, but it had basically the same prices. There was also a jewellery store that had items from $100 to $5,000 a jewel. There was another shop that specialised in Colombian emeralds. Your mom entered and immediately ran out due to the absolutely absurd prices. The prices of the drinks at the bar were also rather high, for example: a piña colada was $6.50 (plus an obligatory $1 tip). Everywhere, there were waiters ready to take your drink order. The only thing your mom wishes that she could have done is to have dined with the Captain. All of her friends had told her that it was a very fine affair, and that everyone dressed very elegantly in tuxedos and long dresses. There was, however, no dinner with the captain. In fact, the only dress-code was that men should wear trousers, not shorts, during dinner. I will send you our photos soon. A hug from Pa.
On every trip I ever went on, I learned many things, so:

Lesson 19. Plan to travel throughout your life, it's like being in university where you experience and learn the facts of life.

<u>Overview of lessons</u>

1. In any sport and in all aspects of your life, be humble when winning and be humble when losing.
2. Even if you are the weakest competitor, there is always a way to win the game if you have a plan.
3. You should always pray, through thick and through thin. If you pray, God will grant you whatever you ask of him.
4. A lesson from my dad, to be honest you must seem honest.
5. Do not spend your life separated form your family from very long, it is to be enjoyed together.
6. A lesson from your Grandma Elvia, always be prepared for everything you do, nothing should intimidate you and always remind yourself that someone will be waiting at the station for you.
7. A lesson from your Aunt Veronica, be the best at what you do, and be grateful to your mother too.
8. Each one of you do whatever you want to do as long as you have defined aspirations and the perseverance to succeed.
9. To succeed in life you must study hard in school and always get good grades; record in your mind that it is essential that you should pursue a career in college and even study a master's degree and then a doctorate.
10. To marry trust your intuition, heart and God. Meet the family of the groom or bride. The moments of happiness in dating are duplicated in marriage. Moments of arguments and fights quadruple in marriage. Pray that God will help you when deciding to marry.
11. A lesson from your Aunt Milagro: "when it is time to have children, do not have only one, ask God to have at least two.'.
12. When drinking liquor and eating fish you must be very careful. Be sure to never drink an excess of liquor.
13. Never fight with your brothers, love your brothers and always communicate with them to solve any problem between you and your brother or sister.

14. Pray before bedtime and you will sleep well. Practice sports, eat wisely, never drink liquor in excess, in your senior years take a small glass of red wine nightly and practise tennis or gold every single day.
15. Sing to, dance, to, learn and most importantly enjoy music.
16. You shall love and respect your parents above all things.
17. Do not spoil your child with material things; enrich them with spiritual gifts instead.
18. Try and organise an annual family reunion.
19. Plan to travel throughout your life, it's like being in university where you experience and learn the facts of life.

About the author:

Marco A. Egoavil Suarez' resume:
Consulting and Troubleshooting of problems in Mechanical Engineering with the use of dynamic computer codes on the following topics:
• Subsonic Combustor, rockets and scramjets.
• Heat and cooling flows in combustors, scramjets, Ramjets.
• Flow Characteristics in the input and output of thermal machines
• Study of boundary layer in areas of intense combustion
• Analysis of flame stability, flame walls with overheating and possible melting analysis by high temperatures.
Professor of Projects in Mechanical Engineering, use of dynamic computer code FLUENT and adviser of theses and dissertations.

Marco A. Egoavil Suarez' industrial experience:

- 1989-2002 NASA Langley Research Center Hampton, VA

- Aerospace Technologist who:
  - Created methods and solutions to problems in structures with mass flows for designing wind tunnels,

- pressure machines, rockets, scramjets, high temperature nozzles, combustion chambers, primary and secondary ignition, injectors.
  - Initiated and developed special projects requiring complex mathematical models and control algorithms for flow systems in thermal systems, using computer codes fluid dynamics. Solutions and results used by a team of engineers served to make key decisions.
- Summer 1988 NASA Lewis Research Center researc associate. Cleveland, Ohio.
- A member of a team investigating "catalytic combustion of fuels rich" and "Effects of turbulence in the combustion of fuel Jet-A". Summer 1987 U.S. Arnold Air Force Station Tennessee.
- A member of a team investigating "Scaling laws of 2D Nozzle Plumes" and "Design of a Mechanism to Control Levels Turbulence in Wind Tunnels."
- Summer 1986 Lawrence Livermore California Research associate.
- A member of a team investigating: "Forced Ventilated Enclosure Fires" and "Salt Modelling of Forced Ventilated Enclosure Fires".
- 1973 Northern Indiana Children's Hospital, South Bend, Indiana. Project Engineer.
- In charge of the creation, development and design of electro-mechanical equipment to teach children how to walk.
- 1955-1963 Compania Minera Agregados Calcareos, Lima, Peru Mechanical Engineer

- Responsible for the design, installation, and testing of mining equipment such as conveyors, belts and buckets, ball mill, roller mill, elevators, grinders, mechanical air classifiers, fans and a vertical lime kiln.

Marco A. Egoavil Suarez' teaching experience:

- 1983-1988 Associate Professor at the University of Puerto Rico Mayaguez.

- Professor of Thermodynamics, Heat Transfer, Radiation, Laboratory of Fluid Mechanics and Thermal Machines Laboratory. 1981-1983 Florida Atlantic University Boca Raton, Florida.

- Professor of Thermodynamics, Fluid Dynamics, Heat Transfer, Thermal Systems and Methodology of Experiments.

- Associate Professor at 1969-1972 Private University Ricardo Palma, Lima, Peru.

- Program Director of Mechanical Engineering, Senior Professor of Thermodynamics 1965-1969 National Engineering University, Lima, Peru.

- Thermodynamics Associate Professor, Supervisor Installing a Laboratory of Thermal machines such as steam turbine, diesel engine, Otto engine. 1964-1965 National Engineering University of Lima, Peru.

- Assistant Professor part time teaching Machine Design.

Marco A. Egoavil Suarez' education:

- 1981 University of Notre Dame, Notre Dame, Indiana PhD. Mechanical Engineering.

- University of Illinois Urbana-Champaign; attended classes on Internal Combustion Engines, Gas Turbine Design, Fluid Mechanics Laboratory course.

- Technical Teacher's College Wolverhampton, England; attending classes on how to teach courses in Mechanical Engineering.

- Thermal Sciences Field.

- 1961 University of Notre Dame, Notre Dame, Master of Mechanical Engineering.

- 1954 National Engineering University of Lima, Peru, Mechanical Electrical Engineer.

- HONORES 1959 Scholarships: Fulbright and Smith Mundt to study at the University of Notre Dame.

- UNESCO Fellowship to study pedagogy courses applied to thermal sciences field, at the Wolverhampton Technical Teachers College, England and at the University of Illinois at Urbana-Champaign.

My Eleven Grandchildren in 2008

Seated: Kyra, Matias, Ariana, Natalia, Veronica, Lola,
Isabela.
Standed: Jeremy, Grant, Gabriela, Camden.
Colors: Yellow, Strutzels, black, Gerdts', red, Rubios.